Fiction Writing

3 Manuscripts in 1 Book, Including: How to Write Fiction, How to Write a Screenplay and How to Edit Writing

Jaiden Pemton

More by Jaiden Pemton

Discover all books from the Creative Writing Series by Jaiden Pemton at:

bit.ly/jaiden-pemton

Book 1: *How to Write Fiction*

Book 2: *How to Tell a Story*

Book 3: *How to Write a Screenplay*

Book 4: *How to Write Sales Copy*

Book 5: *How to Edit Writing*

Book 6: *How to Self-Publish*

Book 7: *How to Write Non-Fiction*

Book 8: *How to Write Content*

Themed book bundles available at discounted prices:

bit.ly/jaiden-pemton

Copyright

Table of Contents

Fiction Writing..1

More by Jaiden Pemton 2

Copyright..3

Table of Contents..5

Book 1: How to Write Fiction.....................................7

INTRODUCTION...8

CHAPTER 1: STEP 1 - BUILDING CHARACTERS 10

CHAPTER 2: STEP 2 - SHAPING THE STORY THROUGH PLOT DEVELOPMENT 19

CHAPTER 3: STEP 3 - DEFINING THE "WHERE" THROUGH SETTING 30

CHAPTER 4: STEP 4 - SELECTING A POINT OF VIEW....................38

CHAPTER 5: STEP 5 - DEFINING THE "BIG IDEA" THROUGH THEME...42

CHAPTER 6: STEP 6 - DEVELOPING STYLE AND FINDING YOUR VOICE...48

CHAPTER 7: STEP 7 - UNCOVERING THE SECRETS OF GOOD FICTION WRITING..55

CONCLUSION..59

Book 2: How to Write a Screenplay...........................61

INTRODUCTION...62

CHAPTER 1: STEP 1 - DEVELOPING YOUR LOGLINE 65

CHAPTER 2: STEP 2 - BRINGING THE SCREENPLAY TO LIFE THROUGH CHARACTER DEVELOPMENT...................................71

CHAPTER 3: STEP 3 - EXPANDING YOUR SCREENPLAY THROUGH PLOT 83

CHAPTER 4: STEP 4 - GENERATING THE FIRST DRAFT 88

CHAPTER 5: STEP 5 - CRAFTING YOUR PITCH DECK 97

CHAPTER 6: STEP 6 - REWRITING FOR REFINEMENT 102

CHAPTER 7: STEP 7 - APPLYING THE SECRETS OF DISTINGUISHED SCREENPLAY WRITING 107

CONCLUSION 114

Book 3: How to Edit Writing 117

INTRODUCTION 118

CHAPTER 1: STEP 1 - BREAKING EDITING INTO STAGES 121

CHAPTER 2: STEP 2 - READING WORK ALOUD 128

CHAPTER 3: STEP 3 - SETTING THINGS APART 136

CHAPTER 4: STEP 4 - UTILIZING ISOLATION STRATEGIES 142

CHAPTER 5: STEP 5 - INTERACTING FOR DEEPER ENGAGEMENT 147

CHAPTER 6: STEP 6 - LETTING THINGS SIT 151

CHAPTER 7: STEP 7 - EDITING IN REVERSE 160

CONCLUSION 167

More by Jaiden Pemton 170

Book 1: How to Write Fiction

7 Easy Steps to Master Fiction Writing, Novel Writing, Writing a Book & Short Story Writing

Jaiden Pemton

Introduction

There is a magic in storytelling that has been present and passed down from generation to generation. When it comes to writing fiction, you have the entire world at your fingertips, and you can create anything you desire. Fiction allows us to take elements of our knowledge, experience, and passions, and mold a reality for our own. As fascinating as this is, the task itself can be incredibly daunting. If you find your characters falling flat, your setting getting lost in the background, your point of view changes throughout the story, or your theme becoming lost in the chaos, you are not alone. When it comes to writing fiction, there are a lot of things to keep in mind in order to keep the reader engaged and be sure the story is being told in a way that is memorable, meaningful, and easy to follow.

While it can be difficult to discern the best way to channel story ideas into a cohesive fiction piece, the process of fiction writing doesn't have to be as overwhelming and chaotic as it may seem at first glance. All it takes is a deeper understanding of each of the elements of fiction writing. Also, the details that influence how each of those elements unfolds. This guide breaks down the details within each step of fiction writing, opens your mind to new possibilities, and helps you to come in touch with your goals for fiction writing.

The chapters of this guide will take you through each step of fiction-writing in a way that will help you check all the boxes and avoid common mistakes. Each detail is designed to keep you on track and answer any and all questions you may have about fiction writing. These sections contain all the information you need to develop well-rounded characters, a logical plot, an in-depth and meaningful setting, a suitable point of view, and a relevant and influential theme for each fiction story you write. Throughout the journey, you will find yourself discovering your own writing voice, and experimenting with

various styles of fiction writing until you find the one that is the best fit for you.

Each chapter is organized in an easy-to-follow, subtitled format with comprehensive examples of every tip, trick, and technique. This all-inclusive guide to fiction writing also contains a number of special fiction-writing secrets embedded throughout the text, which can help to develop your skills as a writer further. Whether you are aiming to write fiction stories based upon experiences in this world or another, this guide has all the tools you need and is sure to serve as the perfect guide to revolutionize your fiction writing experience.

Happy writing!

Chapter 1: Step 1 - Building Characters

Before you can begin to tell a story, you must determine who the people are that are enduring the story. It is the characters who make the story move—who draw the reader into a new world and make them feel a part of it. The most important part of character development is to make your characters feel entirely real. If the character seems flat, aloof, or unrelatable, your reader will not be able to create a connection with them, and they will entirely lose interest in the rest of the story. Therefore, developing real, raw, and complex characters should be in the forefront of your character developing process. Think back to when you were a child. If you ever walked away from a movie or finished a book and found yourself imagining what your life would be like as the characters, that means the characters were well-developed. Something about the way those characters were represented, even if they lived in a society, era, or lifestyle that was entirely different than your own, made you feel like you could put yourself in their shoes.

Additionally, real and raw characters are more likely to portray the deeper messages of the book because the reader will develop a sense of trust and compatibility with them.

Character Introduction

It is vital to introduce your character to the reader at the beginning of the story so they may begin to develop a strong initial connection. Certain hard and fast details like age, cultural background, nationality, voice, occupation, and markable physical qualities like tattoos, style of dress, beauty marks, or imperfections are important to establish an initial image in the reader's mind. Another way to set characters apart and create individual images for each of them is to give them a tag. Tags are notable qualities such as an accent, a particular piece of jewelry, a unique gesture or mannerism, or a passion unique to that character. If, for example, your protagonist is in love with a girl down the street who has black and white tattoos all the way up her arms, this is not only an initial point of interest but also a distinguishing element of that character to make them stick in the reader's mind and bring back throughout the story. Additionally, the significance of the girl's tattoos can lead to opportunities for dialogue between characters and a deeper representation of the girl's personality and life.

From the beginning, your reader should have enough details to have a distinguished image and voice in their head whenever a particular character enters the scene. Once you have introduced your characters, it is important to establish trust with your reader, giving them credit to use their own imaginations and develop a unique understanding of each character as they read the story. One of the most important elements of fiction writing is "show, don't tell." You should not have to provide a lengthy narrative summary to develop your reader's understanding of the characters. Rather, the character's background story, daily choices, internal dialogue, and the way they orient themselves in the world should speak for themselves.

Establishing Character Depth

After the initial introduction, your characters will continue to unfold into three-dimensional figures. Remember that character development involves creating an entire human being with a past, a present, and a future—you must be thorough. Although you may not reveal every single element of your character's past in the story itself, you must personally be aware of every single detail that composes that character and their experience. Basic descriptions of physical qualities and personality traits are not enough to establish depth. Take a piece of paper, and write out the elements of your character's life from their birth until the present moment. Where were they born? Who are their parents? What did their family unit (or lack thereof) look like? What sort of impact has this had on their development? What is the relationship status of this character? Do they work or attend school? Do they have any children? Who are the people in this character's circle; do they have a best friend? What are this character's hopes, dreams, skills, and talents? What most commonly produces an issue in their everyday life or stands in their way?

You should establish a personal awareness of what triggers anger, fear, grief, or trauma in this character, and why that is so. It is also important to assign a personality type to your character. Is this character a peacemaker who sometimes struggles to put their own needs first, or are they constantly ready to speak up, challenge authority, and fight until they are heard? Perhaps this character is a deep creative who feels largely misunderstood by the world, or a timid, rule-abiding personality trying desperately to find their own voice.

Making Characters Relatable

It is impossible to identify or empathize with any character who does not possess human qualities. This means you must have a basic understanding of human psychology, how people's brains work, and what causes people to react to things the way they do. If, for example, your character possesses superhuman strength, is kind at all times and never runs out of patience or energy, has no physical flaws, or never experiences emotional conflicts, your reader will not feel that they can relate. Humans are imperfect and flawed, and conflict is a regular aspect of our lives. It is important to keep this fact in mind when you approach fiction writing.

Your character should have flaws, just as every human being does. However, because your main character must possess some heroic qualities, you must ensure that these flaws are forgivable, identifiable, and easy to empathize with. It is important to dedicate plenty of time to define your character's flaws, how these flaws impact their lives, and how they move beyond (and in spite of) them. Your character will struggle, but they should never be portrayed as weak or cowardly. Although they have flaws, there should always be heroic qualities present that keep your reader engaged and rooting for character growth and success.

Growth as Expressed by the Character Arc

In terms of growth, it is vital to understand the "character arc". The character arc represents the path on which a character grows and changes throughout the story. Just as human beings are constantly changing as a result of what we learn and experience, so it should be for fictional characters. Throughout the story, great attention should be given to the character's inner dialogue. What keeps your character awake at night? Do they have any secrets? What is their largest fear, shame, and driving force? At the end of the story, what does your character know about themselves or the world that they did not know before? How has their life changed as a result of what has happened to them? How have they grown as a person? How do they approach the future?

In the book *The Alchemist,* for example, the young shepherd boy begins the book striving for something greater but feeling unsure of how to get there. Throughout the course of his journey to find the treasure, he is met with insights on his interactions with other people, the fire at the heart of every human being that can act as a guiding force, and the presence of omens to guide people towards that life purpose. His character develops until he has made the pinnacle observation of where to find the truths of life and oneself.

Making it Personal

When it comes to fictional character development, it can be helpful to take personal inspiration. Consider the complexities of your own life, personality, and those of the people you know. You can take the approach of changing several details of a personal experience to create a new circumstance. What are some ways that particular circumstance could have turned out? How do you wish it went? Could it have gone worse? In fiction, you have the freedom to base your characters off of real people in real experiences, while changing as many details as necessary to create your own story. We will take more about personification in later chapters.

Writing Exercise: Putting Yourself in Their Shoes

One of the greatest joys of writing fiction is the freedom to embody the characters you create. Whatever you dream of being—the villain, the heroine, someone of a different personal or cultural background, a mystical creature, a young child, a single mother, a soldier—fiction gives you the space to be that person. Every time you sit down to write on a certain character, take a few moments to close your eyes, breathe deeply, and truly become that character. At every twist and turn of the story, ask yourself, "what would I do if I were in this character's shoes right now?"

As you develop your characters, ask yourself which words you can use to summarize that character's personality most accurately. Are they bold and confrontational or shy and reserved? If the character is bold and aggressive, you may write about circumstances in which they stand up for the ones they love and fight for the underdog when no one else will. However, their confrontational nature may also get them into trouble when they grow passionate and have trouble controlling their abrupt reactions. Putting yourself in your character's shoes can guide the events of the story, as well as the character's growth. In the case of the bold and confrontational character, perhaps they feel that in order to be strong, they must not be soft in any way. Over the course of the story, their character arc may involve learning about the strength that lies in being soft and allowing their guard to come down sometimes. In the case of the shy and reserved character, their journey may involve learning the strength in their own voice and how to use it to influence change.

Establishing Character Credibility

A final important detail of character development is establishing credibility. Although fiction writing gives you the freedom to make your characters whoever you want them to be, you will not be able to develop them without some research fully. If you are writing a character who comes from a different personal or cultural background than your own, has a different passion or occupation than your own, or has experienced a tragedy that you have not. It is not enough to base their story off of simply what you imagine it might be like. To create a well-rounded character for your readers to fully understand and empathize with, you must literally put yourself in that character's shoes. One way to do this is by finding interviewees who have had similar experiences to your character and can answer questions to generate a deeper understanding. If you are writing on an ER nurse, for example, you could try calling into a local hospital and asking for an ER nurse who would be willing to book an interview about a day in their life. Begin by asking the interviewee to describe a typical day in their life, doing the things the character in your book will be doing. Develop several questions to serve as a guide, then follow up with further questions as the interview goes. Be prepared to be surprised and confront ideas you were not prepared for. All of those details are important to include in order to establish true character credibility.

Another great option is to go into an environment like that of which your character lives or works in. In the case of the ER nurse, you may want to try to schedule a day to go into that environment and shadow an ER nurse on their day at work. Take field notes of everything you observe. You may even find that you can draw further inspiration from the specific details of that setting and the people you see there. You can go into any neighborhood, classroom, landscape, or other environments with a journal and allow it to move you freely. Write down your observations and any feelings you experience in that setting, and channel them into the description of your characters and their lives.

Chapter 2: Step 2 - Shaping the Story Through Plot Development

As you take on the beginning steps of fiction writing, you will often find that plot development and character development happen subsequently at times. The plot feeds heavily off of the characters navigating through it. And how they develop from the start of the story to the end. When planning out the specifics of what happens in your story, there are several key questions to ask yourself. First of all, you should identify a primary sequence of events and how your characters change over time as a result of those events. What locations does each of these events happen in? How does each of these events contribute to the larger structure of the story? How does it do with the development of its characters?

The Importance of the 5 W's (Who, What, When, Where, Why)

The 5 W's are one of the most important clarifying factors of any story. You should establish straight away who the important characters are, where the story is unfolding when the story is unfolding, what situation the characters are in, and why they ended up there. The best stories are not only clear about each of these 5 W's; they also provide room for circumstances to change. You can further engage your reader by demonstrating changes in the who as your protagonist finds a new part of themselves and unlocks new strength. Another example of engaging your reader in the who of your plot is if one of the characters turns out to have an identity. They have been hiding that is revealed later on in the story. This may bring an element of surprise to the reader and cause them to shift their perspective. Perhaps the where may change as the protagonist gets a new job or moves to a new city. You can also change the what by detailing revelations your character has about what their true goal in life is. Take as much time as you need to generate thorough answers to these questions.

Plot Development Toolbox: Outlines, Timelines, and Storyboards

In the beginning stages, you may find it helpful to create an outline that provides a detailed summary of how the book flows and how each event is connected. It can also be helpful to create a comprehensive timeline of events in the novel, which can later branch off into separate chapters. Storyboards are an excellent tool to keep you on track as you move through each of the story's scenes. On note cards, post-it notes, or something similar, you can detail which of your characters will be involved in each scene, and what the main point of that particular scene is. You will then have the opportunity to reorder the scenes as the story develops until you end up with the most logical sequence. As you transition from the planning process to the actual writing, you should be able to describe what the story is about using only two sentences. Once you can do this, you know that your ideas are fully developed, and the story has a strong foundation on which to be built.

Plot Introduction (What's the Main Goal?)

As you begin to introduce your characters at the beginning of the story, you must also introduce the plot by making the reader aware of each character's main goals. Be specific in describing these goals. For example, it is not sufficient to say that your protagonist wants to be a writer in the future. What kind of writing does she want to do? Does she hope to live in a certain area? How do her dreams impact the way she envisions herself in the future? It is far better to say that she wants to be a famous poet, living alone in a mountain cottage, and traveling the world, than simply that she wants to be a writer. The main goal should be established as a driving force to the character's life—it is the most important thing to them. This goal will shape why the character chooses to act the way they do. What decisions do they make? How does their goal motivate them and define their daily life?

Be sure that any main goals you present are realistic and attainable. Remember, you want your characters to be established as human beings first and foremost so that the reader can relate to them and empathize with them. Leave room for the story to continue developing and for the main goal to expand and change after the protagonist is faced with conflict. Large-scale plot development should be fueled by the basic, everyday moments the characters experience. You can reveal a lot about the underlying themes of the story by giving small details such as how a character engages in dialogue or what sorts of simple actions they take (such as how they make their commute in the mornings or how they decorate their desk).

Exposition

This crucial introduction to the characters and their motivations occurs in the exposition. The exposition is the first part of plot development, in which characters are introduced within an established setting. There should be some explanation of the primary themes and main events of the story. The central conflict should be evident from the beginning, and it should draw the reader in and make them want to know what happens next. The exposition will introduce whether the structure of the story is linear or non-linear. Linear structure is chronological—it starts at the beginning and builds from there. Non-linear structure, however, drops a reader into a moment right in the middle of things. This gives the reader a chance to understand the central conflict in terms of what is going on. But not why it is happening. If the story opens with a woman next to her unconscious boyfriend at a hospital, the reader comes to know both characters and that they are in the hospital. But the readers do not understand how they got there. Non-linear structures can create added tension by introducing effects before causes, and this approach can be very engaging for readers, making them hungry for answers.

For the purpose of exploring these elements of plot, let's consider the classic story *The Three Little Pigs.* In this story, the exposition of the plot is when all three pigs are introduced in the setting of the countryside. It is clear in the beginning that each pig has one goal in mind: to build their own house. From the beginning, we know that one pig is building their house of straw, one is using sticks, and the third is taking their time to build a sturdy house of bricks. We are introduced to the main goals and potential themes from the very beginning when we see how the pigs who use straw and sticks are in a hurry to finish building so they can just have fun. The pig who uses bricks, however, is patient and takes the necessary time to develop a sturdy house that can endure much more. Due to its rudimentary nature as a children's story, this story follows the linear structure.

Rising Action

The rising action is the place where everything begins building up to the turn of events. This is where the reader will understand the why and the what that was introduced in the exposition. The protagonist will be faced with conflict, which will lead them to the realization that their immediate goal will not be as simple to obtain as they originally thought; then, the character must begin to establish a New Goal. The rising action portion of the book should be tense and engaging, and the reader should begin to understand everything that is at stake for the protagonist. Character-driven scenes can be used to demonstrate what is at stake. An example of this would be a mother who is trying to shield her daughter from finding out she has magical powers in order to protect her from being discovered by forces of evil who will use her powers for themselves. Character-driven scenes lead to intense action scenes that keep the reader on the edge of their seat, rooting for the main character's success.

In the example of *The Three Little Pigs,* the Big Bad Wolf is introduced as a dangerous character who wants to eat the pigs. He watches them build from afar, plotting when he will attack. It is at this point in the story that the reader understands the why behind the pig. The pig who chose to take the time to construct a sturdy house of bricks. When the big bad wolf arrives, the pigs who built their houses of straw and sticks are faced with conflict (the Big Bad Wolf trying to break in and eat them, then blowing their houses down). This leads them to understand that their immediate goal, to build their houses quickly and return to business as usual, is not as practical as they thought. This part of the story contains the intensity necessary in the rising action part of the plot as the story approaches the climax.

Climax

The climax, or turning point, is the point in the story where the protagonist realizes what they must do in order to resolve the conflict. This is the part where the main questions the reader has developed throughout the course of the story are answered. At this point, all of the tension and emotion that has accumulated throughout the first part of the story will be released. This is when the story switches from building conflict to conflict resolution, and it is often the most engaging part of the story. It is important to keep readers on the edge of their seats by making them question whether or not the protagonist will come out on top and experience a happy ending. There should be some element of doubt present—a moment where all seems lost before the protagonist rises above the challenge and ends up on top. The climax is the point where the reader develops an even deeper admiration for the main characters as they observe the characters making brave decisions, learning an important lesson, persisting through challenge, and rising above.

Using our *Three Little Pigs* example, we see the emphasis switch from the main goals of the straw and stick pigs to the main goal of the brick pig. This is the part of the story where the brick pig becomes the hero by allowing the other two pigs into the sturdy brick house. Tension continues to mount as the wolf tries to blow the brick house down and fails, then begins plotting another way in. At this point, the brick pig exhibits vigilance and quick-wittedness while preparing for the Big Bad Wolf's next move. When the Big Bad Wolf attempts to come down the chimney of the brick house, readers are left on the edge of their seats, wondering if he will get in and eat the pigs after all. However, in the end, the brick pig is too smart, and the Big Bad Wolf is encountered by a pot of boiling water in the fireplace. The Three Little Pigs are safe at last—a happy ending in which the characters learn an important lesson about being patient, thorough, and smart.

Falling Action

Everything that occurs after the climax is part of the falling action. The falling action should be in alignment with everything that has happened, leading up to that point, and it should feel inevitable. It must be directly tied to decisions and actions made previously, and the outcome should seem logical. This is the point where all the primary questions have been answered, and all conflicts have been resolved.

There are several versions of *The Three Little Pigs,* but one example of a falling action that can be seen in some of them is when the pigs engage in singing and dancing after the Big Bad Wolf has been defeated for good. As they dance around, carefree and enjoying themselves, the reader can see how the pig who made a house of bricks was right — patience is key. At this point in the story, all of the pigs are happy, safe, and unified together, and they are all benefiting as a result of the third pig's decision to build a sturdy house of bricks for protection, then place water on the fireplace to outsmart the Big Bad Wolf.

Resolution/Denouement

The final aspect of plot development is resolution or denouement. This draws all events, conflicts, and questions to a conclusion. This is the place where all of the loose ends are tied up by the lovers finally ending up together, the hero receiving recognition, or the adventurer returning home. This part of the book symbolizes a new, and generally improved, reality for all of the characters. At this point, the characters will have undergone great development as well and will have grown into wiser and improved versions of themselves who have successfully resolved the conflict they faced. This part of the story should be logical (do not introduce outlandish scenarios or new characters here) and leave the reader feeling satisfied.

The recognition the third pig receives in The Three Little pigs when the other two pigs express their gratitude for being protected and apologize for judging the third pig for working at a slower pace, is an example of resolution. At this part of the story, the reader can truly see how it all paid off and how the other two pigs have grown wiser and learned from their mistakes. Ultimately, the reader should arrive at this resolution feeling satisfied that all the pigs are safe, happy, and have learned a new life lesson.

The Use of Subplots

Although subplots are not the main idea of the story, developing subplots can be useful for supporting the main plot and highlighting the most crucial issues and themes at the heart of the story. An example of a subplot could be the protagonist's relationship with the shop owner down the street who always shows grace and kindness and holds space for people to share about their life issues. The development of this relationship over time could serve to drive in the story's key points about human relationships and a general understanding of the kinds of people the characters are.

Clarifying Questions: Did Your Plot do its Job?

As you approach the end of your story writing process, it is important to go back and ask yourself several important questions to ensure that you have stayed on track with what you wanted to express in the plot. Have the characters changed over the course of the story in the way you hoped they would? What were the key areas of growth or learning for the characters? What led them to change? Did they achieve their goals? Lastly, did you stick to the core themes of the story (for example, true love always prevails)?

Going back once more to *The Three Little Pigs* example, the goal of the story is that taking your time to think things through will benefit you later. We can see that this has been clearly demonstrated over the course of the story in the way the two pigs who did not take their time learning from the third pig, who did. This is an area of character growth and learning for the pigs. It is also an area of triumph for the pig who was not afraid to go against the grain. At the end of the day, the third pig's goal, to live in a house sturdy and safe from dangers like the Big Bad Wolf, has been achieved. The theme of the story has been achieved by demonstrating how patience and thinking things through led to a happy ending for the pigs.

Chapter 3: Step 3 - Defining the "Where" Through Setting

In order to draw your readers into the world you create in fiction; you must first have a profound understanding of what makes that world what it is. This is where developing a setting comes into place. When it comes to writing fiction, there is often much emphasis placed upon who the characters are, what they are doing, and what is happening to them and very little emphasis on the environment they are in. The setting is one of the most widely overlooked yet equally crucial components of fiction writing.

Basics of Setting: What to Do and What Not to do

Before setting out to develop your story setting, there are several things to keep in mind. First, when describing the setting, it is important to use all five senses. By describing exactly what the characters can see, hear, smell, taste, and feel, the reader will feel completely immersed in the story and where it goes next. The setting is not something that you can establish once and expect the reader to stay engaged throughout the rest of the book. It is important to spread setting descriptions out throughout the book in order to pull your reader into each moment truly. Whenever the plot is thickening or changing, and the character's actions need to be emphasized, that is a good time to provide new details of the setting.

While in-depth sensory descriptions of settings are crucial, there is a fine line between being thorough and over-describing. If you spend too long describing every tiny detail of the setting all at one time, your reader is sure to lose interest and become distracted. Not only this, but over-describing a setting may also stifle a reader's imagination, making it more difficult for them to envision the world in a way that is captivating to them.

Location, Context, Social Era, Lifestyle

Now that you are aware of how to approach the setting, let's talk about the details you'll need to provide in order to illustrate the bigger picture. First of all, you need to know the general location of your story. This involves the country, region, city/town, or planet (if your story takes place in another world). Once you have established a general location, you will break it down into smaller categories such as specific neighborhoods, households, or places of work or study. It is important to establish context around the social era the story is taking place in as well. If the story is happening during a post-war era, or in a city neighborhood that is being newly gentrified, those elements will greatly impact the journey. The journey of the characters and the unfolding of the plot. You must take into account any element of culture. What country, tribe, or community are your characters involved in? Do they have any special family traditions? What are the foods they eat? It is important to indicate the general social and political climates of the story, as well as how people interact with one another in different contexts.

Geography and Population

Geography is an element of setting that goes hand-in-hand with a location as it pertains to the natural environment. Does your story take place in a mountain village, off the coast of Mozambique, in a corner of East Harlem, or in a galaxy far beyond our own? You must make your reader aware of both natural geography (oceans, rivers, forests, mountains) and man-made geography (bridges, monuments, buildings, cemeteries). Also, to be taken into account with geography is the population of a given setting. The character's experiences are likely very dependent on how many people live in their area. The experience of a character living in a small town, versus a city with several million people, versus an isolated island, will all be vastly different.

Climate, Mood, Atmosphere

The climate of a setting goes along the same lines as its geography as well. It is important to establish the relationship between climate and people's moods and well-being. It is more common, for example, to see a relaxed and carefree lifestyle in a village community on the coast than in Seattle on the 200th cloudy day, or in the deep woods while a family struggles to survive during a harsh winter. The mood and atmosphere of a story are developed as the characters react to elements of their environment, including temperature, lighting, and other factors that can be detected by the five senses. Before each scene, be sure to take time to ask yourself what kind of mood you are striving to establish. What is the weather like? Is it sunny and serene, with puffy clouds in the sky? Or is it a gloomy day with whistling wind that makes the hairs on your arms stand up? If the story is occurring inside, what is the atmosphere of the room? Is it comfortable and cozy, or is there something unsettling about it?

Time of Year, Time of Day, Passage of Time

Time of year is another important element of setting, which includes seasons as well as important days. These days can be holidays, first days of work or school, or significant dates to the characters such as anniversaries, birthdays, dates of death, and dates of past historical events. Time of day is important for describing if events are happening at dawn, dusk, in the heat of the afternoon, or in the middle of the night. While it is not possible to take the reader on a moment-by-moment journey as it would be in real-time, it is absolutely crucial to account for elapsed time throughout the story. Flashbacks, foreshadowing, and in-between moments can all be used to allude to the passage of time and keep readers from becoming confused or feeling removed from the story.

Establishing Setting in Fictitious Worlds

In the cases of fantasy and fictitious worlds, you will have a bit more work to do in order to draw your reader in and make them feel connected with the setting (as it is a world they have never seen). Begin by creating the world your story is occurring on. Does it resemble earth in any way? What are the major differences? Establish the name of the world, as well as how its creatures live and function. What is the terrain like? One very helpful tip for establishing this fictitious world is to draw a map. After you have developed a map of this world, you can narrow things down and determine in which particular settings the plot will unfold.

Why is Setting Important?

One common misconception about the setting is that it is only the backdrop of the story. This is incredibly false. The setting is crucial to the development of a story because it includes everything that has to do with how the characters navigate through space, time, and social environments. Think about the places in your own life where you spend the most time, for example. If you spend most of your time on a college campus, it is likely that you have a favorite meal in the cafeteria, a favorite faculty or staff person who you look forward to talking to a favorite tree or bathroom stall, and a favorite place to study. It is also likely that there is a building or room that you rarely enter because it is rumored to be haunted, or because the meanest or creepiest staff or faculty person works there. This is just one example of how setting impacts the way we orient in the world and why it is so crucial to creating a good piece of fiction writing. Every component of the story setting is essential to building the mood and plot of the story. As well as how the characters grow and change within each context. Your setting should be clearly described using literary devices and descriptive language that can clearly draw a picture in your reader's mind to help them envision the environment.

When story setting is done right, it will help the plot to flow from one event to the next clearly and realistically. The story setting should align with the plot of the story. For example, if you are writing about a young musician who is struggling to get by and make it big in New York, you will want to describe the setting of his closet-sized apartment. Also, the streets where he feels unseen and the subways he falls asleep on every day as he travels home from the barista job that barely pays the bills. A rustic, mountain setting would not make sense for this plot.

Further Benefits of Setting

The setting also creates a sense of unity between the characters and the plot by describing why the characters do what they do and which elements of their environment lead them to be in certain situations. Additionally, setting draws the reader in to feel like they are truly in that place with the character, experiencing the same narrative and emotions.

The setting should be aligned with the main characters throughout the story. Going back to the example of the young musician. If his conflict is being withdrawn and not having the confidence to pursue his dream, it is likely he keeps his eyes down on the city streets and attempts to sit alone and mind his own business on the subway. However, if he is outgoing and willing to talk to anyone or do anything to fulfill his dream, even when that means failure, it is likely he is trying to talk to everyone and drop his name in any context he can. He may be trying to instigate conversations about his music with everyone he comes across and is likely to seize any opportunity to perform (at parks, in cafes, in bars, etc.). In this case, the character's conflict would not be a lack of confidence, but rather, lack of opportunity or being noticed.

Establishing Setting Credibility

Just as it is important to establish credibility with character development, it is important to develop that same credibility with the development of particular settings. If you are trying to describe a real place that you have never been, it is crucial to do research on that place to make sure what you are describing is geographically and culturally accurate. If it is a place you can visit in person, that is the best way to get a real-life understanding of the setting. However, this is not always logistically possible. In those cases, you can make use of media resources such as Google Earth, YouTube, newspaper clippings, images/photographs, and encyclopedias. You may also do the same thing you did in the stages of character development, where you visit particular settings and take field notes on what you observe.

Chapter 4: Step 4 - Selecting a Point of View

The point of view of fiction writing is the type of narration you choose to tell the story. When it comes to selecting a point of view for your fiction story, you have several options to choose from.

First-Person Point of View

The first-person point of view adopts the perception of a character, generally the main character, of a fiction story. This point of view records everything as it is witnessed and understood by the character, and uses pronouns such as I, me, and mine. This point of view is useful for giving the reader a closer look inside the mind of the character, letting the reader know exactly how they think and feel and allowing for a more personal connection between the reader and the character. This close connection is a major benefit to using the first-person point of view. One disadvantage is that you may not be giving your reader a well-rounded view of the setting and the other character's perceptions of things. This point of view is more personal but also more limited.

Second-Person Point of View

In the second-person point of view, the narrator speaks directly to the reader and adopts pronouns such as you, your, and yours to tell you your own story. In fiction writing, second-person is most commonly used to guide the reader through interactive books.

Third-Person Objective Point of View

Third-person objective point of view is when a character serves as the narrator of the story but without any insight into their personal thoughts, feelings, and perception of what is going on. This point of view aims for neutrality through the use of third-person pronouns, and it is designed to be unbiased and give the reader the freedom to interpret what they are reading freely without the emotional response of the narrator.

Third-Person Limited Point of View

Third-person limited point of view uses both third-person pronouns and insight into a particular character's emotions and perception of the world. In this point of view, all characters will be referred to in third-person, but only one (usually the main character) will be followed throughout the story from start to finish.

Third-Person Omniscient Point of View

Third-person omniscient point of view is focused on giving the reader a point of view similar to that of a godly figure, looking down on everyone else and seeing what is happening. This point of view provides deep insight into the personal lives of several characters throughout the book, not just one character. In order to write in this point of view, you must be prepared to provide details of the emotional states, inner dialogues, perceptions, and actions of multiple characters.

Dialogue vs. Narration

When thinking of how to write a point of view, you must understand how to use the tools. The tools of both dialogue and narration. Even if the narrative is being written in third-person, first-person pronouns are still used when dialogue is occurring between characters. This is why it is crucial to symbolize every phrase of dialogue with quotation marks to set it apart from the rest of the text.

Point of View Toolbox: Moods and Dimensions

There are several tools available to you when deciding which point of view to use in a piece of fiction writing. Begin by asking yourself what type of story you are writing, and which sort of mood you hope to create. If you are writing a story designed to be suspenseful, you will be better off writing from a first-person perspective, as it is more limited and will inevitably create more tension. However, if you are writing a fantastical story about another dimension, you may choose to write from several third-person perspectives in order to give the reader a better understanding of the world.

Using Your Own Voice

The point of view you choose is also largely dependent on the journey of finding your own distinct style and voice to use in your writing. In order to develop your own strong writing voice, be sure to pay close attention to the differences in voices and points of view in the fiction stories you read. Ask yourself how you perceive different points of view differently. Which one sticks with you the most as a reader? While it is helpful to use the voices of other writers as inspiration, it is important not to attempt to imitate any other author's voice or force yourself to use any particular point of view. Trust your instincts. You know your story better than anyone!

Clarifying Questions: Observation vs. Participation

Several important questions to ask yourself before beginning are as follows. First of all, do you want your narrator to be involved in the events they tell about? Perhaps they are simply an observer of those events or are serving to reconstruct distant events with their narration. Is the narrator far removed from the story, or is there a lot at stake for them personally in the way things unfold? Lastly, is the narrator credible in telling the story? Can your reader trust that they have enough information and experience to portray the story accurately?

Chapter 5: Step 5 - Defining the "Big Idea" Through Theme

When it comes to fiction writing, every story must have a deeper meaning. When the reader reaches the end of the story, what is the message or topical knowledge they will be taking away? If your story lacks a theme, it inevitably will be lacking the ability to establish meaningful connections between the characters and the plot, and the story itself will lack significance or memorability. The theme is a central element of fiction writing; it answers the question, "What is this story *really* about?". Before you proceed with a piece of fiction writing, you should be able to summarize the main purpose of your story in one sentence. One important distinguishing factor is that theme is not the same thing as the moral of the story. The moral of the story is a lesson the author wants the reader to take away, while the theme relates more heavily to the deeper significance of the story.

Major Themes in Fiction Writing

The most powerful themes are generally those which appeal to common interest or understanding. The theme "good trumps evil" is one of the most common themes in literature, which expresses that even when the battle is challenging, forces of good always come out on top at the end of the day. The theme of power struggles and dynamics are also popular, and such themes typically demonstrate that one must have secret powers or approaches in order to achieve dominance. A common theme is one that claims the freedom of humans and the challenges of living in a society that tries to limit that freedom. Contrarily, there is a common theme that expresses society as the saving grace. That protects humans from their natural, animalistic wickedness.

Determining Your Theme(s)

Choosing a theme depends heavily on the general audience you are writing to, as well as the genre you are writing in. For example, the writings of romantic novelists would revolve around themes of love. Begin by determining the broad themes you plan to discuss (love, loss, power, loneliness, family, coming-of-age, self-discovery, mystery, the pursuit of happiness, etc.). You may determine that you want to write a cross-over of several themes, for example, the relationship between the pursuit of happiness, loss, and self-discovery. One way to maintain relevance to the theme is to base it heavily on your characters, setting, or plot. For example, if your protagonist is a professional female swimmer training to qualify for the Olympic team, your themes could have to do with competition, drive, the sport of swimming as a whole, the challenges that face women in athletics, or any combination of those. Ultimately, the theme is a summary of all the primary ideas of a story. Many great stories explore a variety of topics and subtopics, but it is important not to go so broad that your reader gets lost. A good rule of thumb is to select anywhere between two and five primary themes that your story will focus on. This will help you avoid getting off track and will keep your reader engaged. Lastly, although themes will vary between genres and intended audiences, it is important to select themes that are relatively universal and can appeal to people of all races, genders, cultures, lifestyles, ages, etc.

Thematic Statements

Thematic statements based upon opinions or moral discoveries the characters express throughout a piece of fiction writing which communicate a deeper message to the reader. The thematic statement is what combines and summarizes the main topics of the book in a brief phrase. For example, if the themes of a book are love and equality, the thematic statement could be "love your neighbor as yourself." Thematic statements demonstrate how the theme plays out in the world. After you know what your thematic statements are, you can stay on track with the larger purpose of your story and eliminate the details which don't support that larger purpose. It is important to keep character arc in mind when developing thematic statements in order to draw the reader in with a sense of humanity. Thematic statements can be present in everything from the character's backgrounds to their current internal conflicts. When writing about your character's experiences, it is vital to ask yourself, "How is this experience going to impact the reader? What message is the reader going to take away from this?"

The Use of Motif

A motif is a symbol, structure, or literary device that is recurring throughout a piece of fiction writing. Geography is one primary example of a motif. The themes in a story about a girl living on a Polynesian island and a teenage boy growing up in Baltimore, for example, would be very different. The elements of geography can play strongly into the reiteration of the theme throughout a story. Another common motif is the weather, and how changing weather patterns can represent a change in mood and expression of the theme.

The Use of Symbol

A symbol is a particular object, image, figure, or character that represents a deeper meaning. An example of a symbol is the bow and arrow Katniss uses in *The Hunger Games*. While on the outside, this is an object used in battle, it is also a symbol that represents the depth of Katniss' stealth, skill, precision, and courage.

The Relationship Between Theme and Character Development

As previously mentioned, a large part of theme development is dependent upon the character arc. It is vital to consider how the character's experiences, opinions, and morals relate to the overarching theme of the story. When considering the timeline of scenes and character interactions, it is important to ask yourself how they all contribute to the overarching theme. If your theme is "the concept of marriage," for example, and is focused on a young woman learning the lessons about marriage that the other women in her family never learned. It makes a lot of sense to provide a scene exploring her relationship with a single mother character who left her husband after he was unfaithful.

Staying on Track

One of the biggest benefits of summarizing your primary themes from the beginning is that you can refer to it as a guide throughout the rest of the process (and subsequent development of motifs, symbols, and characterization). There is nothing worse than a piece of fiction writing that jumps from one scene to another in a chaotic manner that leaves the reader with questions and leaves them unable to identify the point of the story. Establishing your main themes ahead of time can help you avoid adding secondary characters, subplots, and random details that do not relate to what you are trying to convey. This skill, also called "cutting the fat," is necessary for keeping your reader from becoming lost, frustrated, or bored. Another useful tip for staying on track is to incorporate the primary theme(s) into your outline process, so you can have extra assuredness that each scene you write is relevant.

Because the theme is so dependent on other elements of fiction, such as the characters, plot, and setting, it is rare that writers are able to understand their theme from the beginning fully. Although you do want to establish primary themes to serve as a general guideline throughout the writing process, you may find that your theme will shift slightly as you go. If this happens, you must be prepared to re-evaluate and make adjustments accordingly to ensure that everything still flows.

Out of the Box Tip for Theme Writing

As previously mentioned, it's good to be able to summarize what your story is going to be about, and what some of the primary topics are, before you begin writing. That being said, many writers may find it inhibiting on their writing process to try to determine the theme before the story has even begun to take its course. In some instances, you may find it helpful to give yourself a brainstorming session in which you write down all of the possible topics and theme possibilities that lie within your story idea. You can loosely tie the primary topics into your planning process to keep you on track, but allow yourself some flexibility to let the main theme(s) of the story appear as you go. Although you will begin with some general ideas of what you want to express and what you want the reader to take away, it is a great idea to let the process guide you into creating a more concrete definition of your theme. Allow yourself to move with the flow of the story and watch how your theme(s) appear to you.

Chapter 6: Step 6 - Developing Style and Finding Your Voice

The writing world is brimming with possibilities for self-expression and stylistic variation. The voice and style you develop in your fiction writing allows you to create worlds all your own, which can serve as reflections of your inner world and personal aspirations. When it comes to developing your personal voice and style in fiction writing, there are several important things to consider. This chapter will explore the most crucial elements on the journey of finding your personal style and voice.

"Show, Don't Tell" with Style and Voice

As previously mentioned, it is important to leave room for the reader's imaginations by describing scenes with enough detail to both draw the reader in and inspire them to draw their own mental pictures. However, when it comes to developing style and voice, the way you choose to "show" is crucial. You should try to think outside the box when generating descriptions that stray from the typical perspectives. Ask yourself, "how can I apply my own personal twist to this perspective?" Another tip is to utilize expressive vocabulary. When using common adjectives, such as "beautiful" or "exciting," try searching for synonyms that can express the same thing in a more colorful way.

Determine What Makes You Unique

Every person sees the world in a different way. Perspectives are formed through life experiences, and because every person has a different story, every person has a unique perspective. No matter how insignificant you may feel your perspective is, it is guaranteed that there are elements of your perspective that can provide a new way of understanding the world to your readers. A good starting question when it comes to defining your personal voice and style is: "what makes me unique?" You may find it helpful to create a list of things that contribute to your perspective and who you truly are, from which to draw your personal style in writing. If you are a typically "romantic" person, allow that perspective to infiltrate your writing and create romantic storylines with your own unique twist. While your unique qualities may be as broad as a particular personality type or passion, they may also be narrow, such as your quirks, habits, guilty pleasures, strange fears, special objects, obsessions, or what brings you comfort. Allow the unique qualities you notice in yourself and other people to play a role in the way you detail the characters in your story. Perhaps you are writing about a character who wears glitter on their eyelids every day, has a nervous habit of shaking their pen when they or thinking, or who has a trademark way of greeting people. As mentioned in the Character chapter of this guide, such qualities are endearing and help the reader to build a personal connection with the characters in fiction writing.

Be Authentic

When you allow yourself to be completely authentic in your writing, you will quickly distinguish yourself as a writer. Some writers are known for writing with an element of suspense. At the same time, others write from a mystical perspective or explore the depths of the feminine. The sign of pure and engaging authenticity is to draw readers in so far that they forget what they are reading is fabricated. Over time, this engagement will lead to increased fiction writers developing their own unique presence in the writing world and becoming known for what they bring.

Be Original

Another crucial element to establishing your style and voice is to avoid clichés. If you are trying to imitate another storyline or style of writing, your writing will be dry and unoriginal, and it will ultimately lose the reader's interest. It is important to trust your own experiences and perspective enough to let it guide your writing process and avoid clichés. If you find yourself writing a phrase or following a storyline that seems like something you have heard before, it is a good idea to choose another direction to travel in.

Activating the Senses

One of the key elements of discovering your voice and personal style is to integrate sensory experiences into your writing. In order to draw your readers into the story, you must write in a way that illicit emotion and floods your reader with imagery to keep them engaged. To appeal to your reader's senses, you must write in a way that appeals to your own. When illustrating a scene, ask yourself what the character sees, what they hear, what they smell, and what they feel. As human beings, we are all attuned to different details of daily life. This personal attunement gives writers the ability to describe two very similar experiences in a completely different way, thus immersing the reader in a sensory experience unique to that author's perception of things. Allow your personal attunement to certain things to fuel your writing process and set you apart.

Spicing Things Up with Metaphor

A great way to unleash your creative side in fiction writing is to create metaphors out of everyday objects. This exercise can be applied to any object in your line of vision. Ask yourself about the backstory of that particular object, giving it a past, present, and future. Ask yourself, "What could this object stand for beyond its general purpose?" Consider, for example, a chipped coffee mug on the shelf of a thrift store. Day after day, people come in shopping for mugs, but every time they pick up this particular one, they end up putting it back because it's chipped. When someone eventually decides to purchase the mug in spite of the chip, this could serve as a representation of giving new chances and finding the value in brokenness.

The Importance of Intimacy

The more you invite the reader into a written experience, the more of an impact your writing will have on that reader. Your descriptions of setting and character should include minute details, which can help place the reader even deeper in the story and help them to feel like they are part of it. Seemingly insignificant details, such as the sound of the wind rustling and the branches of a tree brushing against the upstairs window, help the reader to put themselves in the character's shoes and experience the emotions the character experiences. Intimate details are another tool for distinguishing your writing style and truly bringing the reader into your world.

How Personal Experience Influences Voice

A common misconception among writers is that in order to generate fiction, you have to stay far away from any experiences that resemble your own. In reality, quite the contrary is true when it comes to fiction writing. Personal experience can serve as an excellent starting line for the journey of a fiction story. From here, you can draw inspiration from real people, emotions, life memories, and personal philosophies. Writing from this place creates space for empathy and authenticity in the story, which is sure to draw readers in and allow them to build an emotional connection with what they read.

Not only can you base some characters, elements of plot, setting, or theme, off of things you have experienced in your life, fiction also gives you the freedom to change details or elaborate in any way you choose! In fiction writing, you have the opportunity to use your personal life as a basic guideline, then let your imagination get to work in carrying the rest of the story. There is plenty of room for imagination and theoretical situations in relation to personal experiences, and the best fiction writers take advantage of this and allow it to influence their personal style and voice. Because every person's life is unique, so then can the way those experiences impact their writing.

Practice Writing Every Day

Coming to terms with personal experiences, memories, dreams, and philosophies is not a simple process. Humans beings are incredibly complex and constantly changing based upon what happens in their lives. One of the best ways to sift through experiences and find what you strive to express in your writing is by participating in writing every single day. When you sit down to write, try to do so without any expectations or plans in mind. Allow yourself to free-write without paying attention to any of the typical rules of writing. Allow your soul to pour out on the page, then allow yourself to be inspired by what comes from it. Over time, you will begin to notice recurring themes, philosophies, and passions, making an appearance in what you write about. Your free writings can serve as inspiration for the situations your fiction characters experience and the lessons they learn.

Chapter 7: Step 7 - Uncovering the Secrets of Good Fiction Writing

Now that you have covered each of the elements of fiction writing. You are almost ready to be on your way. However, any writer can follow the tips and information provided in definitions of each element of fiction. It is not by simply following the previous steps that you will become a strong and memorable fiction writer. In order to become truly distinguished, there are a few secret techniques to bear in mind.

1. Read, read, read. The more you indulge in personal reading endeavors, the more you will be able to identify the elements of fiction in practice. You will become familiar with the literary devices, style, and voice used by various authors. Pay attention to how certain stories make you feel and what you take away, and approach each of your own projects with the energy you hope to make your reader experience and what you want them to learn.

2. Dare to ask yourself, "What if?" and "What next?" Dare to dream about what you can create in your fictional world. If 'X' happens, what will happen to 'Y'? Give yourself space to think of all possible outcomes.

3. Take risks and immerse yourself in new environments. If you stay in the same place, doing the same thing, the writing you can base upon your personal experiences may begin to dwindle. Challenge yourself to try new things and visit new environments, and take notes each time you do. How might the observations of this new environment create a unique story idea?

4. Give yourself time to soak in the process. As writers, it is easy to feel a rush to get new stories generated as quickly as possible. This can be a critical mistake. In order to create a story that will stick with the reader, bring joy to your soul, and enrich your experience as a writer and a human being, you need to have the patience to let yourself ruminate in the writing process. This can come by way of sitting in quiet and pondering past memories and experiences of your life, which are fueling your stories, daydreaming about mystical worlds from which your story settings are drawn, or simply sitting at the moment and letting images and ideas flow freely onto the paper. Not only will giving yourself time and being present make your personal experience more enjoyable and lifechanging, but it will also refine your story and make it a true masterpiece.

5. Aim to write what has never been written before. Every writer has the capacity within themselves to create something

completely unique using their personal style and voice, but this takes courage. You must be vulnerable with the parts of yourself that long to come to the surface. Allow yourself to engage with them and let them flow forth in your works. Learn from your own process, be inspired by what comes. This is the only way to inspire others with your writing truly.

6. When you are describing scenes in fiction writing, pay attention not only to the descriptive words you use but how they flow together. Language has the ability to create rhythm with the way it flows together. Read your descriptive sentences aloud, changing words as needed until the rhythm and sounds reflect the mood.

7. Maintain an obligation to yourself. Although the goal of a writer is always to keep readers engaged, the primary goal at the end of the day should be to yourself. How can you write the stories that are on your soul? How can you say the things that you have been given the words, experience, and passion to say? At the end of the day, what your writing does for you personally is the most important thing.

8. Life is about choices, and life stories are no exception. Before setting out to write any story, consider the series of choices the characters will make. Why do the characters make certain

choices, and what impact do those choices have on how the story unfolds?

9. Determine particular "writing spaces" for yourself. Each time you set out to write, ask yourself where you need to be. You may take inspiration from writing in a garden, on a rooftop, in a junkyard, next to a country road, hunkered at a corner table of your favorite coffee shop, or settled at a writing desk you have created for yourself with things that inspire you. No matter where it is, make sure that you are in a space where your surroundings can inspire you and put your mind and spirit in the place they need to be.

10. Just get started. You may find yourself writing ten, fifty, or several hundred pages that don't end up going anywhere. That is part of the process. The hardest part of creating a fiction story is often simply choosing to get started. Decide to do that, and give yourself grace and patience as you observe where the process goes from there. Mistakes are a crucial part of the process, and you often have to sift through a lot of ideas and type many words before realizing where you are really trying to go.

Conclusion

Throughout this guide, you were provided with the ins and outs of fiction elements, including the basic elements, things to avoid, and tips to apply to your writing process. At this point, you not only have an interest in writing fiction that inspired you to start these 7 steps, but also the tools to embark on the journey that is fiction writing.

At the beginning of this guide, you learned how to develop characters with whom readers can relate and establish emotional connections. You learned how to add depths to characters and to make their personal growth journey engaging for the reader. Next, you learned about the elements of the plot, and how to prepare your story by establishing a character's main and new goals, conflict, and eventual resolution that leaves the reader feeling satisfied. You learned that setting is not just something that sits in the background of the story, but rather an incredibly dynamic force in the way the story plays out. You learned how to discern between the various points of view and how to select one based on your purposes. You then explored the possibilities of theme, and how to stay on track with what your story is truly about. After this, you examined how to cultivate your personal writing style and voice, largely depending on your past experiences and personal values. Lastly, you were provided with ten out-of-the-box secrets for improving your fiction writing.

This guide is not the endpoint of your journey to fiction writing— it is just the beginning. Now that you have familiarized yourself with the elements and secrets of fiction writing, you can continue to use this guide as a map; you refer back to throughout your process. Now is your time to change the world through the worlds you create in fiction writing.

Book 2: How to Write a Screenplay

7 Easy Steps to Master Screenwriting, Scriptwriting,

Writing a Movie & Television Writing

Jaiden Pemton

Introduction

There are thousands of ideas for screenplays floating around in such a booming industry, and directors, producers, managers, and executives don't have time to get through them all. The industry is cutthroat, and therefore it is crucial to develop screenwriting skills that set you apart and get your screenplays into the hands of the right people.

It can be easy to find yourself writing screenplays that are too much like what already exists when it comes to screenwriting. You may struggle to get producers to read past your logline, and even if they do, you may find that engagement is lost before the play has come through to the end. It is easy to fall into the trap of using clichés, creating boring dialogues, or being too predictable in the unfolding of events. When it comes to screenwriting, there are several elements to keep in mind to ensure that your audience is engaged and that your story will live on with them and distinguish you in the industry for years to come.

Screenwriting can seem like a daunting task, especially in today's age, where thousands of people are trying to make it in this industry. That being said, all screenwriters still hope to discover the elements of their experience that set them apart and can be tapped into to create one-of-a-kind screenplays. All it takes is an in-depth knowledge of screenwriting aspects that will make producers, managers, and audience members alike care about what is being told to them and want to stick around for the shining moment.

This guide will serve as your step-by-step reference through the realm of screenwriting—breaking down the details within each step of the process and helping you to understand what makes legendary screenplays.

The chapters of this guide will take you through each step of screenwriting in a way that will help you check all the boxes and avoid common mistakes. Together, we will explore the best techniques for catching attention, developing characters, developing plot, creating dialogue, writing first drafts, conducting revisions, getting started, and staying on track. Each detail is designed to keep you on track and answer any questions you may have about the screenwriting process.

Each chapter is organized in an easy-to-follow, subtitled format with comprehensive examples of every tip, trick, and technique. This all-inclusive guide to screenwriting also contains a few exclusive secrets and information that can further develop your skills and create impactful screenplays. No matter what sorts of scripts you aim to write and who you are trying to appeal to, this guide has all the tools you need and is sure to serve as the perfect guide to revolutionize your storytelling experience.

Happy writing!

Chapter 1: Step 1 - Developing your Logline

Like most writing pieces, you must know what kind of story you wish to tell before beginning your screenwriting process. When it comes to screenwriting, the phrase that answers the question: "What is this about?" is called a logline. Traditionally, loglines have been printed on screenplays' spines to allow producers to get an idea of what a screenplay would be about. The logline was ultimately what helped producers to decide if reading the script was worth their time. Today, while the logline is not always printed on a screenplay's spine, it serves the same purpose through verbal communication or along with a treatment (which we will discuss in a later section).

The logline is used to summarize the story, typically in a single sentence, and it strives to convey the thesis, tone, and emotions of your story. The standard word count for a logline is about 30 words, but some cases are exceptions (some complicated screenplays need a logline that is several sentences).

Setting the Precedent

Your logline should provide some insight into what happens in the story and the style in which it will unfold, and how the audience should expect to feel. Within the logline, you will also set a precedent for both your protagonist (the hero/main character) and your antagonist (villain/rival). There are four essential elements to a solid logline, which are as follows: Introduce the protagonist, the incident that triggers a reaction, the goal of the protagonist as they deal with the experience, and the central conflict the character faces. Regardless of which order these things are mentioned in, it is vital to ensure that your logline addresses all four elements.

Identifying the Protagonist

When you identify the protagonist, it is crucial to include detailed descriptions of their physical attributes, personality, and life story. After you have mapped this out, choose an adjective and proper noun combination that accurately describes them. If you are writing a screenplay about a poet named Annie from New York who spends her days working in a bakery and takes the subway to the same hole-in-the-wall speakeasy to perform her work and learn from other poets, you may describe her as a "fervent poet."

Inciting Incident/Triggering Action

The next step after identifying the protagonist is to describe the incident, which triggers a reaction. This is the catalyst for your screenplay; it is the event that gets things going. What is the thing that comes into your character's life and completely changes everything? This incident can be either positive or negative; whichever you choose, make sure it is drastic.

In the case of the poet, let's imagine a positive triggering incident. Let's imagine that one night at the speakeasy, a well-established poet from Atlanta called Blaire stumbles in and is so wowed by what she hears from Annie that she asks to take her on as an apprentice and help her publish her first collection. For the logline, this event needs to be summarized in several words, such as: "when she receives the offer of a lifetime from a well-established poet from Atlanta."

Defining the Protagonist's Goal

Another crucial element of the logline is the protagonist's goal. Whatever that goal is, it will serve as the force around which all other activities in the story revolves. This can be expressed in the logline by describing to the reader what it is that the protagonist needs or wants. Annie's goal, for example, is to be a successful poet. That is what she wants; it is the reason she works a day job at a bakery and takes the subway across the city to a hole-in-the-wall speakeasy even on her most tired days, gets home late at night to eat a microwave dinner and write a few lines before bed, and ultimately, take the opportunity to move to Atlanta for the opportunities she sees for herself to be an apprentice and become published.

Creating a Central Conflict

The final element for drafting a successful logline is to present a central conflict that inflicts a sense of excitement and emotion. What possible obstacles may keep your protagonist from achieving their goal? These obstacles can be people, relationships, physical, psychological, or emotional challenges, etc. Is Annie going to face conflict because she misses New York and is flooded with challenges in Atlanta? Will she struggle because she catches feelings for Blaire and no longer knows how to maintain a healthy work relationship? Does she have to leave Atlanta because of it? Or perhaps, she and Blaire kindle a relationship which directly impacts Annie's success, especially as Blaire becomes abusive and controlling of her, and she feels trapped in a city far away from any support system.

Brainstorm several possible conflicts, select the one that is most high stakes, and summarize it using only a few words. An example of this would be "a perilous romance." The following serves as an example of a logline for Annie's story: "When a fervent poet from New York gains the unexpected opportunity for her next big break, she moves to a new city, only to be swept up in a perilous romance that could either make or break her career."

Gaining Visibility and Holding Attention

Screenwriting is incredibly competitive, and as such, there is no time to wait to grab producers' attention. Because the logline is often the first thing a producer looks at, crafting a great one could be the difference between you and thousands of other aspiring screenwriters. For most screenplay competitions, film festivals, and further showcase opportunities, it is the logline that determines whether your screenplay will become accepted.

Therefore, the logline is one of the most important aspects of becoming accepted to opportunities to gain visibility as a screenwriter and get your work out there to producers and executives. Producers, managers, and agents are flooded with script ideas and do not have time to dig into each one's details. This is why a good logline is so important—it is the thing that may catch their attention long enough to implore them to read your script.

Summarizing your Pitch

Another benefit of writing a good logline is how it can help you summarize your pitch, that is, the way you will present your screenplay idea to other people. The more engaging your logline, the more attractive your pitch will be. The confidence and concise nature with which you describe your screenplay is crucial to capturing and keeping the audience's attention.

Master Tips for Crafting your Logline

Use action words to describe what happens. Make sure the language you choose can be easily transferred to actions on stage or screen. Be unconventional. Make it clear from the very beginning that what happens in this story is something the reader will not be able to predict—compel them to come on the journey of this screenplay, and let them know they are in for a wild ride.

Hook your reader with a dramatic narrative. Draw them in but do not give away the ending-- leave them on the edge of their seats, with no choice but to read the rest of the script.

Chapter 2: Step 2 - Bringing the Screenplay to Life Through Character Development

When it comes to bringing a screenplay to life, it must have fully developed and wide-ranging characters. As human beings, we all have different life experiences, passions, speaking styles, and general presence in the world. All of these are things that must be taken into careful account when it comes to character development. When developing characters in screenwriting, you must consider the physical and personality characteristics that are distinctive to that character and what motivates them in each scene of the screenplay. Is this likely to assume a position of leadership in particular situations? Do they fade into the background? Is the character a pessimist, optimist, caregiver, jokester, narcissist?

Aligning Characters with Theme

The characters you develop should be directly in line with the story you strive to tell and the story's message. What is that story about, and how does each person involved play a part in bringing it to fruition? When you develop your logline, you ultimately are deciding on the theme of your story as well. How do your characters align with that theme, and how do their actions influence how the reader or audience perceives the theme? There must be characters who are in conflict with the central question and who have to experience a significant change in themselves to realize the answer.

Establishing Interest and Empathy

It is important to draw all qualities of a character together to determine the voice they take throughout the screenplay. You must be sure to maintain a level of empathy and fascination with each character. As you plan out each of your characters, ask yourself the question: what makes this character interesting? Going back to Annie and Blaire's story, let's imagine the thing that makes Annie interesting is the way she writes poems about people on the subway and values her career as a poet above everything else.

Annie is willing to sacrifice sleep, food, and stability in the pursuit of poetry, and she shows persistence in the way she will stop at nothing to get there. Imagine that Blaire is cool-headed and stumbled into success without meaning to. She has an electrifying presence that draws people to her like magnets and keeps them there. When it comes to the empathy piece, you should be sure that each of your characters has some sort of reason or motive for the things they do. Even if your character makes a poor choice or addresses the story's antagonist, there should be some level to which the reader or audience members feel they can understand. There should be something that has happened to the characters who do bad things or make poor decisions that explain why that character does what they do (even when it is unjustified).

Show, Don't Tell

When it comes to character development, you must be able to show, not merely tell. Say to the reader that a particular character is kind and generous but never demonstrates any situations in which they choose to give of themselves to others or treat other people with kindness. There will be no credibility established between the reader and that character. In each line of dialogue, a particular character speaks, their motivations should be clear, and the actions they take should be even more precise. Remember, when it comes to screenwriting, actors will eventually perform physical actions on stage. Be sure to write to accommodate this.

Defining Character Purpose

As you develop your characters, ask yourself the purpose that character exists for in the story's scheme. Do you have a depressed mother who lives to show parents' reality trying their best for their children and yet still struggling to rise above? Is the daughter character someone who learns to demonstrate compassion towards her mother's character, despite the injustices of having an absent parent?

Or does the child assume an attitude of defiance, decide to end the relationship, and promptly leave her mother one day? Each character's position in each scene should contain a more profound message, truth, or perspective that is shown to the audience through the action and dialogue of that character.

Character Archetypes

When it comes to the details of character development, it is essential to consider character archetypes. A caregiving character, for example, is not going to be the selfish character of the story. They are likely to be kind, nurturing, and there to support other characters throughout the screenplay. These are believable actions for them to take. In contrast, selfish, narcissistic, or cruel actions are not reasonable and may throw the reader or audience members off if they are overused. For each character, you develop and write out a full character description, including how that particular character is related to the protagonist and what role they have on the protagonist. It is a good idea to sketch out your characters ahead of time and read over them several times until you have developed the most exciting plot points and conflicts possible.

Use of Dialogue

One of the most distinguishing factors of screenwriting as compared to other types of writing is the use of dialogue. Through dialogue, readers and audience members come to fully understand the characters and what they serve to represent within the screenplay's message.

As you develop how your characters will orient in dialogue, keep in mind the power of various speech patterns and speaking styles. It is essential to imagine all of the details of how actors should speak when portraying particular characters. What speed do they speak at? What are their tone and inflection? Do they have a specific catchphrase?

Just as human beings are unique and have different backgrounds, upbringing, and perspectives, so should your characters. Dialogue is the tool through which you will demonstrate various upbringings and perspectives as your screenplay unfolds. A young male gymnast in Russia, a child who lives in New York and spends her days being a caretaker for her siblings, an older woman who loved through the Great Depression and now lives in a retirement home in the suburbs, a woman who has grown up in a tribe in the Amazon rainforest, and a man living at a mental hospital after being disowned by his family will all have very different ways of speaking, viewing the world, and ultimately, influencing the track of the story. When you develop character dialogue, it should represent the place that a person comes from, the time period, and the things they experienced in their past.

Providing a Back Story

The dialogue between characters should serve to provide readers and audience members with necessary information about the character's backstories. Through dialogue, the audience members should come to understand what motivates the characters to react the way they do. Your audience members should be able to walk away after production and describe how a particular character would respond in a hypothetical situation. If you have ever had conversations with your friends about "If I were a character from ______ who would I be?" that screenwriter did an excellent job of creating distinguished characters with whom you could establish a connection and demonstrate your understanding of that character's personality.

Using Monologue

If your screenplay uses monologue at any point, it is vital to make it stick out. Monologues are most useful when they demonstrate some elements of character development. An example of this would be if Annie realized she was in an abusive relationship, had a monologue with herself one night in the shower, came to the realization that she had to escape, and then found a way to do so. This demonstrates the development of her character, as she finds the strength and courage to leave, as well as the development of the story as a whole.

Distinguishing your Characters

When characters are engaging in dialogue in a particular scene, there must be distinguishing factors that allow you to understand who is speaking. Well-developed characters are characters the audience member can identify simply by their style of speaking and their approach.

As you design your characters and determine what distinguishes them from one another, try to quiz yourself by covering up character names and seeing if you can identify who is who simply by their actions and how they engage in dialogue. Once you can do this, you can be sure that you have developed complex characters who each serve a purpose and are necessary to the story in their own right.

Using Character Complexity to Create Surprise

Another benefit of developing complex characters is that there is more potential for shock value. Does the person experience a mid-life crisis that leads them to flee home and go across the country? Are they kind throughout most of the play and then end up having a breakdown and become evil? Or perhaps they start out evil and have a change of heart. Whatever the case may be, you can use characters and how they change throughout a show to connect your audience to the message further and surprise them throughout.

Crafting Multi-Dimensional Characters

One last thing to keep in mind when it comes to character development is that the characters you develop should have many dimensions, just as human beings do. Think of yourself on a given day. You may have a great day one day, where you are joyful in everything you do, engage in meaningful conversations, fulfill all of your obligations, and treat people with kindness. The next day, you may be anxious, or angry, absentminded, or simply unable to keep up with everything going on. We all have good days and bad days, and dimensions to our personality which impact how we act in a given social scenario. The characters you develop in your screenplays should be just as complex. What are the traits that are characteristic of them, and what features are uncharacteristic and symbolize that something is off? Make sure to establish these things early on in the character development process. What is the mood of each character in each scene, and how does it change throughout?

Tips for Character Writing

One of the best tips for character development is to develop a personal connection with the characters. Many successful screenwriters dedicate a lot of time to considering all the possibilities of personality traits that may exist within a given character and how that character may react in certain life situations. They do this so much that they eventually reach a point where they feel like they know the character on a personal level.

Another option is to brainstorm a variety of characterizations based upon major life events each character endures. In some cases, it can help draw inspiration for personality or physical appearance based on other characters you have seen or other people you have known. If you have a photo to use as a "model" of your character, this can also be helpful.

Another standard method is to write character outlines or create diagrams that demonstrate how multi-faceted characters are. Suppose you're writing about an antagonist who originally comes off as a kind person and an ally. In that case, you may create a bubble map diagram in which the character's name is in the middle, and branching off from that are other bubbles with characteristics such as "manipulative," "deceptive," "sneaky," "dishonest," "intelligent," etc. all which lead to the tactics this character uses to appear reasonable while working towards their harmful agenda.

Crafting Character Biographies

Character Biography is an excellent tool to make use of when it comes to character development. This writing exercise helps you develop your characters' history from the day they were born until the moment your story starts. What forces have acted on that character's life to bring them to where they are? Did anything happen during their earlier years that led them to adopt certain behaviors? Just as every person you meet has an entire story that has led them into that moment, so should the characters you develop.

Trace that character's journey all the way back to when and where they were born. Who were they born to, and how did their family history impact what sort of situation they were taken into? What city or country were they born into, and have they had to move to a new one or watched the one they always knew undergoing changes? Is the character born male or female? Do they act in particularly gendered ways? Did they have a healthy relationship with their parents? Did their parents have a healthy relationship with each other? How do they align or not align with what is expected of them culturally, concerning gender, etc.?

Did they grow up with siblings or as only children? If they did, what was their relationship like with their siblings? What challenges or successes did they have in school or with extracurriculars? Did they have physical, psychological, or emotional struggles? What did your character learn from the people they grew up around? Have they experienced a traumatic event of any kind? When the story begins, how much life has your character lived? How old are they? Have they moved around or lived in virtually the same place their entire life? Were they born in an area that is different from where the story takes place? Have they had a happy, sad, difficult, or relatively easy life leading up to that point?

It is also essential to consider the various elements of personality your characters have demonstrated over the years. What was their relationship with authority? How did they orient in social situations? Were they respectful, goody two shoes who never got in trouble, or were they always making mischief? Were they social and outgoing, or did they prefer to remain reserved? Perhaps they started out as one and then adopted the qualities of another. No matter what you decide, allow yourself to find joy in the process, and be guided by your creativity. It is also okay to draw influence from your personal life or the lives of other people, you know.

Give yourself time to write about ten pages dedicated to several of your main characters' character biographies in various life stages. Answer as many questions as you can about what their life has been like. How has their personality developed over the years? What strengths and challenges do they face daily, and how does that impact their role in the screenplay events? What are their relationships with other friends, family members, coworkers, teachers, etc.? If the character you are writing about is not the protagonist, what is their relationship to the protagonist? What kind of light do they shed on the main character? If they are the protagonist, what is their relationship to the other people in their lives?

Getting in the Right Head Space

Representing the human experience through character development is not an easy task and it can take time to develop a personal connection with your characters. Give yourself a few days to ponder your potential characters, writing down ideas you have as you go. Dedicate a few hours of undistracted time to brainstorming ideas of how that character might orient in the story. It is important not to judge yourself or be too rigid in the development during the brainstorming process, as it is the part where you simply get to let all of your ideas out without judgment or stipulations. The critical factor here is simply getting your ideas down and coming to know your characters on a personal level. Allow yourself to free write as the characters discover themselves. Who are they in the individual, private, and professional environments of their lives?

Allow yourself to have fun describing the things your character likes and dislikes. What are their passions? What do they like to eat and drink? What is their occupation, and do they like it? What are their current relationships like? In some cases, you may benefit from designing a "day in the life" for your characters and trying to make them as detailed as possible. Allow yourself to discover the characters as you go, much like you would discover yourself or the people you interact with daily.

Think of this as a relationship-building process, like you would experience when dating or building a friendship. You should feel such a connection to your characters by the end that they are like friends or family to you.

Chapter 3: Step 3 - Expanding your Screenplay Through Plot

When it comes to all of the screenplays that exist in the world, it is no surprise that your plot must have things that distinguish it from the rest. When developing character journeys, challenges, and obstacles, you have to be able to think outside the box and go against what people expect. These journeys, challenges, and obstacles look different depending on the screenplay genre, but they must always begin with an inciting incident. As mentioned earlier, the inciting incident is the triggering event that serves as the catalyst into the tensest and action-packed part of the screenplay.

This initial action in the plot is like the doorway that opens and invites the audience into the rest of the story. It is full of surprises and challenges as the conflict unfolds around the protagonist, and the protagonist has to figure out how to address it. At first, the protagonist may feel some resistance to dealing with the obstacle they face. The inciting incident has to be something that takes them out of their comfort zone and causes them to feel hesitant about what to do next. However, the environment must eventually become so high-stakes that they have no choice but to act.

Making your Audience Care

To establish this high-stakes environment, you have to make your audience care about the character and what is happening to them from the very beginning. There is no time to waste; you must immediately establish the emotional connection between your audience and the characters. Help them establish a feeling of hatred, love, or fascination with the character and how life unfolds around them. You have to be prepared to hit the ground running, bringing your reader in so far that once you reach the inciting event, nothing can draw their attention away from what is happening. After you have set this precedent and introduced your inciting incident, you will have established a substantial focus for the rest of your story.

Imagine you are writing a story about a young girl who is learning she has psychic powers. You can immediately engage your audience by establishing a feeling of fascination as they watch the young girl realize she can tell what will happen before it does. She may know that a family of six will move into the house down the street, that the neighbor man will ask her single mother out on a date, that she will see four hummingbirds in the garden one morning, and even that her teacher will be in a car accident on the way to school one day. This builds up the level of fascination within the audience and brings them to the inciting incident.

Setting the First Act

The initial precedent-setting and inciting incident are elements of the First Act, where you must seize your audience and keep them engaged. The central conflict in this part of the screenplay keeps the audience on the edge of their seat, anxious to see what happens in the Second Act. By the end of the First Act, the audience should be very clear on the protagonist's main goals and what is standing in their way.

In the case of the screenplay described, the inciting incident happens one day when the girl gets a terrible feeling in the pit of her stomach and knows that her mother will be fired. Sure enough, when her mother comes into the house that afternoon, her eyes are puffy from crying. This inciting incident leads the girl and her mother to leave the city they're living in and move across the country to live in New York, the place her mother has always dreamt of going. Once the girl and her mother have moved to New York, they face several conflicts, from having someone break into their apartment one night to having roaches and rats in the kitchen, all of which the young girl predicts with her psychic powers. As things continue to go wrong throughout the first act, the young girl becomes increasingly miserable because she can't understand her strengths and doesn't know who to speak to about them. The girl's primary goal is to understand her abilities and learn how to live with them and use them for good.

Introducing Additional Conflicts in the Second Act

Once the First Act Break is over, the protagonist will enter into a place of additional conflicts that pose difficulty to their main goals and bring them towards the climax. At this point, the audience should be able to pinpoint multiple conflicts the protagonist has faced. At the Midpoint region, the character is thrust into an even more challenging situation than they had dealt with previously, and they will have to act differently. This is the point where things seem bad, and the audience will be forced to wonder if the protagonist will end up on top or not. At this point of tension, the Second Act Break will occur. This is when the protagonist has made the realizations and changes they need to make to push the story towards its climax.

The Midpoint region of this particular screenplay could be that the young girl wakes up one morning with the suspicion that there will be a terrible accident on the subway her mother takes to work in the morning. The girl feels desperate to save her mother, and she tears out of her bedroom, only to find her mother has left the house early. The girl finds a note on the kitchen table that reads, "went to the coffee shop down the road before work. Have whatever you want for breakfast; I'll see you soon." The girl tears out of the house and down the street, peering into every coffee shop on her way to the subway system. Her heart is pounding, and the audience doesn't know whether or not she will find her mother.

Tying up the Story with Climax

The climax is the part of the story where everything is tied together, and it becomes clear why everything has happened to lead the protagonist to this point. They have a final confrontation with the central conflict and typically end up on top.

In this story's climax, the young girl races through the city until she finds the subway station where her mother gets on the subway to go to work. She rushes down the stairs and arrives just as the L Train stops and passengers are getting on. The girl sees her mother and begins to scream, "STOP! STOP! There is going to be a terrible accident! Everyone get off the subway!" Most people in the station look at her like she is crazy, but her mother recognizes her voices and turns to face her. Her mother becomes so shocked that she is there that she does not get on the subway.

Instead, the two unite, and the girl begins screaming that they need to leave immediately. They do, and no sooner have they stepped out of the subway than a massive fire breaks out on the tracks.

After this, the rest of the story involves the young girl coming clean to her mother about her powers and beginning to use her psychic nature for good to help the people around her in any way she can (without revealing herself).

Chapter 4: Step 4 - Generating the First Draft

One of the most crucial things to keep in mind when it comes to screenwriting is that your first draft will take on many forms throughout the process of its creation. The first draft exists primarily for your personal use, in truly narrowing down your screenplay's goal and ensuring everything is expressed clearly. Your first draft does not need to embody the final product's wholeness, as long as it contains the essential elements such as theme, plot, and characters. Your first draft can be as basic or as concrete as you wish,

but no matter what, you must be aware that it is not designed to be the final product.

One of the most important things to remember when generating your first draft is this: it is not designed for your intended audience. When you send it out, it should be sent only to those whose advice you trust most, with the knowledge that it will continue to evolve. Allow yourself to take plenty of breaks from the draft, giving yourself a few days to think about other things before looking at it again. You mustn't rush your process. At the end of the day, the first draft's goal is not that it be perfectly polished, but instead that it provides a solid framework on which to build.

Establishing Basic Intentions

As you begin the process of writing your first draft, you should be able to describe the basics of who your characters are, what they want, the obstacles they will face, and the ultimate theme of your story. It is a good idea to start your process with a piece of paper dedicated to your plot, characters, and theme. On each piece of paper, write down your intentions for each of these elements. You can continue to refer back to these pieces of paper throughout your writing process to ensure you stay on track with what you want to express and how you want to express it. It is normal to find that you are straying slightly from your original intentions throughout the screenwriting process. Do not allow this to discourage you—instead, check-in with yourself.

Ask if your intentions still hold or if the story's development and characters take on a mind of their own and lead you towards new purposes. It is certainly okay to adapt your intentions as needed throughout the process of writing your rough draft. The biggest thing you must pay attention to if your intentions shift is that they are all moving in the same direction, so you can make an executive decision to change the intentions without leading certain parts of the screenplay astray.

Writing Detailed Characters

As you plan out your characters, it is crucial to write out all of the details that make them who they are, even if those details are not revealed in the script itself. Even if your audience does not know all of the details of your character's family life, relationship history, favorite things to do, or places where they draw the most joy and inspiration in their life, you should know. You should be able to answer questions about your characters from the most mundane details, like what they like to eat for breakfast, to the profound details, like the dream that they will never reveal to anyone because they see it as impossible. By planning out all of these details ahead of time, you will develop a more real and personal relationship with your characters, and you will find it easier to maintain consistency in their actions and dialogue.

Layering Character Representation

When it comes to characterization, it is essential to ask yourself if these characters are being represented the way you planned for them to be. Are you staying true to their personality traits with the actions they take in each scene? Are the ways they interact with others characteristic of who they are? What are their flaws, challenges, motivations, and goals? How do they fulfill the expectations the audience has of them? How do they veer away from those expectations to surprise the audience?

Throughout the first draft writing process, it is customary to see your characters developing more layers than you initially expected; you may even find that your intentions for each character shift. The first draft writing process is a chance to bring your characters to life, and you may be surprised at the decisions they make and the way they inhabit the story. If you need to, allow yourself to break from the script's goals and write out all of the possible reactions your characters could have to a particular scenario. Give yourself the space to flesh out all of the ways they might feel or react. As you go through this process, try to put yourself in each character's shoes and write from their perspective rather than your own.

Staying True to the Theme

In terms of theme, one of the best ways to keep yourself focused is to ask questions. An excellent question to keep you on track is: What do I want my audience to take forward from this screenplay? Continue referring back to this question as you go, ensuring that what is currently happening will ultimately lead to the desired impact. As you write out the scenes within your plot, be sure to examine the overarching theme of that particular scene and ask yourself how it leads the audience towards a conclusion. How does it make them think? What emotions will it invoke within them? What will they learn?

Taking it Slow

It's easy to lose sight of what you wish to express by giving the first and second acts plenty of time but then beginning to rush as you reach the climax and the conclusion. This can leave the audience feeling deeply dissatisfied and like too much has happened too quickly for them to truly generate an opinion. If you begin to feel desperate to get done but don't have any fresh ideas, allow yourself to take a step back.

Writing the end of your screenplay from a place of urgency and pressure will lead to sloppiness and will inevitably leave the audience feeling unfulfilled. Give yourself time to step away and clear your mind so you can be more thorough and make fewer mistakes when you come back to it. Give yourself a refresher with your initial intentions and ideas. Ask yourself if another film, book, song, or podcast may re-inspire you and remind you why you wanted to write this particular screenplay. It is imperative to give this process adequate time to unfold and refrain from rushing yourself as you start to get closer to the end. Taking this time to refresh yourself early on can save a lot of headaches later, and you'll ultimately be glad you stepped away for a while.

Making Use of Free-Writing

After you have established initial intentions, it's an excellent idea to free-write using a pen and paper or a blank document on your computer. Allow all of the images and possibilities for your characters to flow out freely, without judgment. It may seem strange, but one of the crucial tips for screenwriting is to write the ridiculous and confusing dialogue, unpolished scenes, and random character descriptions. Writing the lousy stuff first makes editing more manageable later on because you have less confusion to work through since you took time to iron out the details beforehand.

Additionally, the more material you have to work with initially, the more potential your screenplay holds. Work through all of your ideas, and see if you can find any common themes. Which images are the strongest? Which connections can you make between them? What opportunities exist for meaningful dialogue? After you have gotten all of your thoughts out, allow yourself to look at them more critically, checking for clarity and being particular about which ideas you qualify to make it into your script. The more ideas you have to choose from, the more likely it is that your script will be fresh and provide something producers, managers, and directors have never seen before.

Setting Attainable Goals

As you write your first draft, it is good to set goals to keep yourself on track. One of your goals may be to write one scene per day so that you can approach each new writing session with a fresh perspective, ready to address the purposes of a new scene. Another goal may be to learn something new from each scene you write and be inspired by the way your script is taking form. You may set a goal to finish writing a scene in a particular amount of time or with a specific tone of the dialogue. Although daily goalsetting is crucial for staying on track, make sure not to overshoot with your goals. Give yourself goals that you can reasonably achieve.

Making Use of Treatments and Loglines

Earlier in this guide, we discussed the fact that a logline is a great way to keep you on track with your script's goals. It is the element that allows you to describe using less than thirty words what your screenplay is all about. This concise summary of what your play is about can be a great reminder to keep you on track as you go throughout the writing process. However, just as there is room for your rough draft to grow and change, there is room for your logline to change along with it. You have to change your logline's wording to summarize your story adequately, especially if you find that your intentions have changed. Allow yourself to make these changes to your logline as needed to stay true to your core intentions and fully capture everything you want to express in your screenplay.

Developing a Treatment

Another useful element of keeping your first draft on track is through developing a treatment. The treatment serves as a more extensive summary of your script's plot, themes, and characters, and it

94

helps bring clarity to these elements. Once you have narrowed down your initial intentions, you can write a piece of prose consisting of several sentences that summarize what those intentions are. The treatment stands between your initial intentions and the actual script and allows you to clarify without becoming distracted by too many extra details. The treatment is brief but provides a little more insight into your particular intentions. In writing this, you can clarify each of your intentions and provide yourself with an objective summation to go back to as you continue to write your first draft. The treatment should contain all the clarification you need to keep yourself from losing sight of where you want to go.

One of the best things about the first draft is that you have the freedom to place as much dialogue as you want. You can allow your characters to talk, however, and about whatever seems fit for a particular scene. However, it is essential to remember that much of the dialogue you write initially will change if it stays in at all.

Fleshing Out Dialogue

As you write your first draft, allow yourself to play into all of the possibilities of dialogue. Inhabit the space of your character's conversations, leaving room for messiness and confusion. What mindsets can you capture using dialogue? Save the cutting and editing of dialogue for the revision process. Once you get to the revision of the first draft, you will have more possibilities to sift through to decide what makes the cut. When it comes time to edit, be prepared to make many cuts to keep the script moving forward in line with the plot, theme, and character goals. If the audience gets lost in the dialogue and things begin to stall, you risk losing their attention.

Maintaining Flexibility

Your first draft is something that should be written with the idea that more versions will arise from it. The first draft is not meant to be even close to the end all be all of your screenplays. Therefore, you should give yourself the freedom to enjoy the process, writing your ideas, and seeing where they lead you. Do not write from a place of tension or pressure to get everything right because that is unrealistic and may slow you down or prohibit you from achieving the revelations that come in letting yourself run free. There is no set number of how many drafts you will produce before you finally reach the end, but you should expect to produce no less than three. Any less than three drafts will leave you feeling nervous, and like there are still ways the draft could improve. Remember, the first draft is only the first step of the journey.

Chapter 5: Step 5 - Crafting your Pitch Deck

As screenwriting has become more competitive over the years, the way screenplays are pitched has changed dramatically. While loglines, synopses, and treatments are still crucial elements of pitching a script, more details are required to succeed in the pitching process. All of these elements combine to create what is called a pitch deck. While the logline is the first thing producers, managers, agents, and development executives will be exposed to with your screenplay, the pitch deck is the thing that will help them go beyond.

Capturing their attention with the logline is only the first part of the process. From there, you must craft a pitch deck which is highly creative, visually engaging, and full of just enough detail and information to make them interested and help them visualize how the story will be told (too much information is not a good idea, as they will quickly lose interest). The pitch deck is the make it or break it factor when it comes to whether or not people will choose to invest in your screenplay. You have to show them why you deserve their investment, what will make your project worth it, and, ultimately, what is in it for them.

When it comes to outlining your pitch deck, you must have each of the following sections: Title page, executive summary, team, story, production, distribution, and finances. Each of these elements will be broken down in further detail.

Catching Attention with a Title Page

The title page will serve as the cover of your pitch and should contain qualities of a poster or similar visual aid. You can share contact information on this title page for producers, managers, agents, and development executives to refer back to. This poster should utilize a color scheme, font, and images that capture your screenplay's tone and atmosphere. You would not, for example, want to use a horror style font on a title page for a romance screenplay.

Providing an Executive Summary

Your pitch deck's executive summary should be one page long and should include your pitch's primary elements. Some crucial information to include is the title, genre, how long the screenplay will be, the proposed budget, and what dates shooting should take place (if it is a film).

Introducing the Team

This section of the pitch deck should include who the prominent team members of the project will be. Team members include attached development executives or producers, yourself, and any co-writers, as well as potential writers, directors, producers, or lead actors if you are pitching a film. Each team member should be complete with an image and a biography.

Telling the Story

To successfully pitch a screenplay, you must be able to provide summarize the protagonist's story and the most important details of their character in a brief but engaging way. Show the reader why they should care about this character and their journey, and how the rest of the world can be impacted. The story element of the pitch deck is the part that includes your logline, which briefly presents your lead protagonist's background and the conflicts they face.

Describing Production

One of the significant parts of the production element is proving to the readers that there are benefits to producing this type of play or film. You can use factors such as demographics, popular interest areas of the general public, current events, etc. This section should also include when and where production will take place.

Building on Distribution

This section gives you a chance to continue building on why this particular genre is needed in the industry and will therefore be a worthwhile investment. Use this section to continue talking about demographics, as well as potential distributors.

Stating Finances

Most projects require money to get off the ground. You must include a breakdown of all anticipated costs for your proposed play or film so that directors, producers, and managers have an idea ahead of time of what their money will be going to.

Final Reminders

There are a few essential things to keep in mind as you develop your pitch deck. The first is to summarize the protagonist's story and the most important details of their character in a brief but engaging way.

Show the reader why they should care about this character and their journey, and how the rest of the world can be impacted by it. Next, your pitch deck must serve to provide the reader with instantly discernable clues. You must use visual, descriptive language, which will paint a picture in the reader's mind of how the screenplay will appear on stage or the screen. Logistically, you need to include complete details about targeted genres, demographics, and financial allocations. You will know your pitch deck has done its job if the reader walks away with an idea of the screenplay's story, character arc, tone, theme, scope, as well as financial and production logistics.

Chapter 6: Step 6 - Rewriting for Refinement

As discussed in the First Draft chapter of this guide, the best scripts are that writers take time away from and then examine with fresh eyes. Screenwriting is exhausting, and it can quickly become muddled. One of the best screenwriting tips is to give yourself at least a week, if not several weeks, of not doing it. Give yourself time to go on a vacation, read a book you've been dying to read, spend some time outside, watch a film or play written by someone else, spend time with loved ones, nap, or anything else you love to do. Allow yourself to clear your mind and pay serious attention to the things happening around you. When you go back to continue the screenwriting process, bring the perspectives you have gathered out in the world back with you. Read your script with fresh eyes, as if you have never seen it before. Be critical in the same way a reader would be, looking for what it is that makes this particular script stand out.

Cutting the Fat

As you work your way through the structure, allow yourself to be ruthless. Toss out the things that do not work out well, and make sure that each scene sets a precedent for what will happen next. Tie up loose ends and clean up messy, unclear areas. Speak the lines of dialogue out loud. Consider the setting dialogue is unfolding in—how does it contribute to the shape of the dialogue and the visual representation on stage or the screen? Check back with the fascination you built at the beginning of the story to measure if your climax is intense and surprising enough. Ask yourself what the audience should get out of this, and make sure their expectations are met.

Developing Compelling Characters and Conflicts

One major mistake to look out for is unengaging characters or conflicts. If your main character is boring and does not keep you engaged, ask yourself what sort of compelling backstory you may be able to give them that might make them more attractive. In the case of the girl with the psychic powers, perhaps an exciting subplot would be that she has previously felt useless and dull as if she brings nothing of much value to the world. This backstory keeps things interesting and retains the character experiencing an element of surprise and rooting for her throughout. In terms of conflict, make sure that it is something that profoundly impacts the character's life. Set the stakes as high as possible, and make sure they are clear and ever-increasing.

In the girl's story with the psychic powers, the stakes reach an all-time high at the climax when her mother is about to lose her life. At this point, the girl's motivations are clear, convincing, and capturing—she must save her mother.

If you find yourself struggling with the story's depth or how the plot unfolds, it may be time to check in with consistency. Ask yourself if the characters are consistent with their intended motivations or how they perceive themselves. Are the instances of each scene engaging but also believable? Can the audience understand why certain things are happening?

Use tools like flashbacks, narrations, or dreams to keep things moving and keep the story from going flat. At the same time, be sure to avoid using too much narrative. If the scenes are too busy telling to show what is happening, the scene will be weak. The goal should be for the scene to be so strong that dialogue can take any shape within it, and the audience will still have an idea of what is going on and what the purpose is.

Avoiding Monotony and Wordiness

Another common mistake to avoid is monotony in the dialogue. This does not have to do with how the lines are being said and the nature of the dialogue. Dialogue should vary from person to person, and each character's lines should be characteristic of their personality and their goals. Remember that character is best shown through action, not through dull recitations of history or exposition.

It is crucial to avoid being too wordy. Every time you approach the rewriting process, you should do so to cut words out of every dialogue and every scene. You should cut the phrases down so far that you are only one word away from the phrase, no longer making sense.

If you are not concise, audience members will become lost in the telling of the story. Remember to show, don't tell. How many words can be replaced by actions?

Avoiding Repetition

If things start to become too repetitive and you find certain scenes or characters being too much like another, take a minute to step back. What are the unique personalities and voices of each character? If you have several of almost the same personality or voice, perhaps consider combining them to create fewer, more interesting characters. Adjust your scene length as needed—if a scene becomes too long, it will begin to seem like everything has already been seen or heard, and it will lose its appeal.

Dealing with Lengthy Scripts

If the script itself is too long, it is time to start looking for areas where you may be repeating yourself. If you have the same information in the script multiple times, it is safe to say it can be cut. You can reiterate information by the actions the characters take, as opposed to having to say it over and over. Check all of your subplots and make sure you are not going in too many directions and trying to cover too much.

Lengthening Scripts When Needed

If the script is too short, it may be a sign that your characters are underdeveloped. You may be lacking a subplot. In the psychic girl and her mother's story, there is room to integrate the subplots about the girl's emotional issues and perhaps her mother's long-time loneliness as a single mother. This adds a sense of depth to the story and gives a lot of room for further development. Be sure not to sacrifice character complexity to keep the plot moving. It is essential to strike a balance.

Reaching out to Proofreaders

Once you've reached the perceived end of your rewriting process, reach out to several people whose opinions you deeply trust. Listen to the way they perceive the screenplay and what advice they give. You do not have to agree with their perspective, but you should take it seriously. Allow yourself to polish repeatedly until the script is no longer improving; it is merely changing forms. Once you reach this point, you're ready.

Chapter 7: Step 7 - Applying the Secrets of Distinguished Screenplay Writing

There are several secrets that every screenwriter should know to create the most engaging, impactful screenplays in the industry. This chapter will serve as a recap of several essential tips to make your screenplay stick out above all the rest.

Fueling Dialogue Through Action and Reaction

As we have already discussed, the best way to draw your audience into a screenplay is to show, don't tell. One great way to do this is to imagine that you are writing a silent movie in which none of the characters can speak. This does not take away the power of dialogue—quite the contrary. Instead, it fuels the dialogue by adding actions and reactions to deliver with the lines. Suppose one character is antagonizing another, and the other character pulls out a gun. In that case, that will inevitably have more power than the character merely saying, "Stand back, or I'll shoot," and taking no action. From this action and reaction, the audience learns that there is great tension between these two characters, and one of them is not afraid to take the other's life away right then and there. Suppose a character dreams of being a famous dancer. In that case, the audience will get more of a sense of her motivation by watching scenes where she dances in her bedroom every night before bed instead of listening to a monologue about how much she cares about dance.

Screenwriting is distinguished from other types of writing in that the content you create is designed to take on physical form on the stage or screen. For this reason, action is crucial to keep the audience engaged with what is happening before them. Think about the events that unfold around you in everyday life. What a bland and confusing world it would be if people did not use facial expressions and other actions along with their words! In many circumstances, it is the nonverbal things that truly express what another person is feeling. By providing actions, facial expressions, and other physical representations along with the dialogue, you can be sure to keep your audience feeling connected to the characters and "reading into" their actions to determine what may happen next.

Determining what Needs to be Said

With every line of dialogue, it is important to look critically and ask if what is being said truly needs to be said or if it can be shown instead. If there is no full reason for it to be said, it is best to cut it out. If you do not find it necessary, neither will the audience. Your dialogue's entire goal should be that it is easy for the audience members to follow along without becoming bored or distracted. Dialogue should accomplish one primary goal: to progress towards the motivation of the protagonist. As you go through your rewriting process, cut your dialogue down as far as it can go.

Make sure that each line of dialogue is serving as a building block to construct the larger picture. With every scene of dialogue, build to the climax and back it up with actions.

Keeping Supporting Characters in their Place

Another tip to keep in mind in terms of character dialogue is not giving lines to the wrong characters. Supporting characters exist for that reason: to support the narrative surrounding the protagonist's goals. Do not make the mistake of having characters talk simply because they are present in a scene. In many cases, it is powerful enough to have a particular character walking around, in silent dialogue with another character, doing their job, etc. while the main dialogue takes place aside from them. Each line of dialogue must serve the purpose of moving the plot and characters forward, and this purpose is defeated if characters are talking just for the sake of talking.

Supporting characters are there to help the lead characters, and they should not speak unless it accomplishes that goal. If their line does not contribute to moving the screenplay forward, the line should be cut. Not all characters in the room need to have a line, and in fact, there is a specific power in having characters present in a scene who say nothing at all.

Concealing Character Desires

A significant way to keep the audience on the edge of their seats is by never giving away what the characters want deep down inside. While the screenwriter should always know the character's goals, motivations, and desires, these things should never be explicitly stated to the audience. Rather, the audience is left to draw their own conclusions about what the characters are striving for by listening to what they say and looking for deeper meanings. The dialogue should never truly reveal what the characters want until the end. This keeps characters guessing and open for discovery, and they will listen more intentionally as they try to crack the code.

"Movie Moments": Speaking Power in Dialogue

One mistake that screenwriters commonly make in writing dialogue is the attempt to make it sound "real." In reality, the best dialogue should not resemble an everyday conversation. The best dialogue should take the powerful form of what people wish they could say but can't. Robust dialogue should not include stuttering or filler words, and it should not go off on tangents. Instead, it should capture raw emotion and be short, assertive ideas that stick with the reader.

Although it is important to include human moments like fragments and interruptions, cinematic dialogue should be impactful, engaging, and sometimes even poetic in nature. As you craft your dialogue, consider what film phrases have become most popular and stuck with people worldwide.

When it comes to writing conflict, you must remember that the best dispute arises from two or more characters with vastly different goals and desires. The conflict should tie itself into every dialogue, which will cause the audience to be engaged with the back and forth, curious to see who is going to come out on top. Inevitably, the audience will agree with one character more than the others and will begin subconsciously rooting for that character's success. Going back to the young girl's story with psychic powers, let's imagine that after her mother comes home from work after being fired and says they need to move, the girl tries to convince her mother otherwise.

At the time, the girl's mother does not know of her daughter's powers and therefore doesn't understand that her daughter is trying to dissuade her from moving because she has a feeling something terrible will happen if they do. The two will go back and forth about why they should or should not move, and at the climax, this discourse will be enhanced by the fact that the little girl turned out to be right— her mother is in grave danger.

Drawing Inspiration from Other Screenwriters

One of the most important things to do is to read other screenplays when it comes to being a good screenwriter. In many cases, writing is all about the inspiration we draw from the most brilliant and successful voices in the field, and screenwriting is no exception to this. Half the battle of being a successful screenwriter is becoming familiar with other people who have already done it.

As you read the work of successful screenwriters, you will inevitably be exposed to stylistic choices, tactics, and approaches that are most inspirational and impactful to the audience. As you read work that inspires you, you are likely to become more inclined to create your work and feel motivated to create something that can impact the world. Frequently, reading other screenwriters' work is just the jumpstart you need to motivate yourself to start your masterpiece. You can experiment with different styles, voices, points of view, dialogic interactions, and character-building techniques based upon what inspires you from the work of others.

Screenplays, especially free screenplays, are like gold to the aspiring screenwriter. Within the thousands of scripts you can dig into, you will discover new ways of crafting dialogue, writing elements of surprise, and keeping your reader emotionally engaged. If you want to improve as a screenwriter, making yourself an apprentice to other screenwriters' work through reading is the best way to do so.

All it takes to engage with thousands of free screenplays is the desire to find them. These screenplays can be found in collections online, and a vast number of them are available with no fees attached. As you read the work of the screenwriters who inspire you most, allow yourself to channel their genius and let it flow into your writing. Artists exist to encourage one another and create a never-ending cycle of creativity, and this is something every screenwriter should use to their advantage.

Conclusion

When you started this guide, you had an interest in screenwriting and the desire to build skills to set yourself apart in the industry. Throughout the guide, you were provided with the ins and outs of screenwriting, how to distinguish your style, characters, and ideas.

You learned how to keep your audience engaged, write meaningful dialogue, and follow a proper screenwriting model. You also learned things to avoid and tips to keep your creativity flowing freely. You discovered how to draw in your readers and keep them engaged and inspire them to invest in your screenplay to bring it to the stage or screen.

You learned how to write a script in an actionable way that is easily transferable to a physical setting, such as a screen or stage. With this, you understood how to keep your readers engaged in the real-world human interactions occurring between the characters. You also came to understand the power that lies in screenwriting and what sets it apart from other writing types.

At the end of the guide, you were provided with expert tips to keep your screenplays fresh and avoid the common mistakes made by amateurs in the industry. You learned how to develop a dialogue to avoids unnecessary details and focus on action. You learned how to determine what needs to be said, and what can simply be inferred through character action and nonverbal cues.

You learned which characters to emphasize and how to avoid the protagonist's focus and their primary goal. Additionally, you realized the importance of reading other screenwriters' work, drawing inspiration, and channeling their power as you develop your personal style, voice, and goals with the screenplays you produce. You began this journey by uncovering the purpose of the story being told all of screenplay writing's technicalities: developing characters, inciting incidents, goals, and an eventual resolution.

You discovered the importance of thorough character development and the use of dialogue, plot development using scenes, and the process of writing drafts and revising to tie everything together. You learned the importance of giving your drafts space and taking time to walk away from the script to allow further creativity to spark new ideas.

You learned how to hook readers and keep them engaged throughout, as well as how to invoke an emotional experience. Additionally, you were provided with comprehensive tips and tricks to help you distinguish yourself as a screenwriter and keep yourself from getting overwhelmed with the process. You learned several key terms and logistical elements of the screenwriting process, as well as tips and tricks for getting your work out in the world and staying there. With this guide nearby as a tool for you to refer back to anytime throughout your screenwriting process if you get stuck, you're ready to begin!

Book 3: How to Edit Writing

7 Easy Steps to Master Writing Editing, Proofreading, Copy Editing, Spelling, Grammar & Punctuation

Jaiden Pemton

Introduction

When it comes to editing, it is crucial to take your time and be thorough, give attention to the seemingly minor details, and interact with the material on a deeper level to ensure the purpose is being fulfilled. No matter which industry you're working with in the writing world, editing is a universal requirement. Whether you're editing your own writing or serving as an editor for another writer, this guide will show you the top-notch editing strategies, which will be sure to set the content you edit apart in your industry and yield ultimate success as an editor.

It is not possible to predict exactly how many drafts you will need to generate before a piece of writing is ready to go out into the world. Ultimately, the more thorough you are, the fewer drafts you will need to generate. The task of editing requires deep focus and willingness to engage with the content wholly to catch the smallest mistakes, inconsistencies, or areas where the text's purpose is getting lost. Whether you are editing your own writing or someone else's, it is crucial to develop skills that set you apart and help you achieve the most accurate and efficient editing strategy.

When it comes to editing, it is easy to fall into the trap of getting bored or exhausted by the content and skimming over important details. You may reach a point where you have looked over the same words so often. You struggle to determine the right word to use when something doesn't sound right or figuring out how to re-instate the purpose.

You may find yourself feeling so eager to have the content wrapped up and turned in that you start missing small details, which can be a vital mistake. As the editor, it is your job to get the piece of writing that is as close to perfection as possible. If your text is full of errors you did not catch in the editing stage, it will push readers away. This guide will provide you with ideas for maintaining your own energy and enthusiasm throughout the editing process and utilizing tactics such as giving the writing space and editing in reverse to keep a fresh perspective.

In this guide you will find a comprehensive step-by-step reference format with everything you need to know about the editing process. You will be provided with in-depth knowledge of the stages of editing, the importance of reading work aloud, how to manage the small formatting details, how to deeply interact with the content to ensure the message is getting across, and creative strategies you can implement to look at the content differently. Additionally, the guide contains excellent tips for keeping your editing process lively and engaged the whole way through.

The chapters of this guide will take you through each step of the editing journey to help you avoid common mistakes and develop your own thorough process. Each chapter is designed with astounding detail to help you stay on track and address any questions or concerns you have along the way.

Chapters are subtitled and easy-to-follow with examples of tips, tricks, techniques, and things to avoid. Regardless of if you are editing your own writing or someone else's, this guide has all the tools you need to set yourself apart as an expert editor and is sure to serve as the perfect guide to revolutionize your editing experience.

Happy writing!

Chapter 1: Step 1 - Breaking Editing into Stages

As an editor, your role is to make sure everything is clear to the reader. If the reader struggles to read the text, either because it is swaying from the purpose or there are too many mistakes with formatting or grammar, they will have a much harder time reaching the end of the piece. Your job is to advocate for the reader by making their journey through the text as easy as possible and ensuring that they are impacted by the text when they reach the end. To increase levels of clarity and consistency for the reader, you must be persistent in the correction and improvement process. Your role as the editor includes correcting the structure, style, grammar, spelling, punctuation, point of view, and information order. Before you begin, it is vital to familiarize yourself with the client's guidelines (if you are editing for another writer) or the publisher.

Breaking Down the Stages

The editing process includes several stages. The first stage is structural or developmental editing, in which you complete a rough copy edit. Line editing and copy editing are the second stages of the process, and the rough copy edit is the result of this stage. The final step is the fine or final copy edit, which involves final proofreading and preparing for the graphic design and "final proof" stages, which will occur right before publication.

In some cases, if the writer has already done a great deal of initial self-editing on the piece, the structural stage may not be necessary, as the work is already structurally sound. If you are writing and editing your own piece, you will need to make plans to send it on to a professional editor to ensure the work is structurally sound, and then again for the final proofreading. This is because, at some point, you will have been looking at your content so much that you will not be able to target any other edits that need to be made.

Stage 1: Structural Editing

The role of the structural editor is to review the writing from a broader standpoint. The structural stage is not meticulously examining the details but instead considering the text's more significant picture issues. This editor needs to be aware of who the target audience is and the author's primary goal. Editors of fiction stories need to ensure that the plot, dialogue, character, and point of view are clearly expressed and follow the same structure. Editors of nonfiction should examination the general organization of the content and question it for clarity and consistency of the argument and supporting evidence.

Scheduling Structuring Consultations

Suppose the structural editor is not the writer of the manuscript. In that case, they will need to consult with the author to discuss the main idea the author is trying to express so they can evaluate it for clarity. Additionally, the author and structural editor should confirm the style manual that is expected in editing. They should be on the same page regarding the style which will be used, which can be defined in a style sheet. The style sheet is a tool for the structural editor to refer back to throughout the editing process, including all necessary rules regarding punctuation, fonts, headings, capitalization, etc.

Once the editor has come up with a list of structural edits, they will need to meet with the author again to discuss the structural improvements and why they are suggesting them. The structural editor may find that the manuscript is structurally sound and does not need many modifications and, therefore, may advise the author to proceed to the copyediting stage.

Determining the Authority of the Structural Editor

In some cases, the structural editor and the author may agree that the structural editor has full flexibility with their changes, including length, word count, number of chapters, or even the point of view. However, in other cases, the structural editor may be expected to consult with the author to receive approval before making any corrections. Another option is for the structural editor to make all corrections as suggestions in a separate draft and submit it to the client so that all the edits made are visible and can be approved or declined.

Increasing Clarity and Consistency

The structural editor must keep in mind that their job is not to entirely change the manuscript but rather, to make it better. That said, they should move and delete sentences or paragraphs only when it is altogether necessary to increase clarity and consistency. The structural editor can make suggestions on switching the order of chapters, creating new chapter sections, adjusting the table of contents, or creating appendices, descriptions, or introductions.

Focusing on the Bigger Picture

Although the structural editor can correct grammar, spelling, and punctuation, this is not their primary focus. The manuscript will endure further stages of editing, which are more dedicated to these small details. The structural editor should maintain focus on the bigger picture. They should be asking themselves if the way the text is set up is easy to follow, if the theme is being clearly expressed throughout the manuscript etc. If the structural editor is different than the editors who will be working on the manuscript in its later stages, they may choose not to correct the finer details.

Stage 2: Line Editing

The first part of copy editing (the second stage of the editing process) is line editing. The line edit is sometimes called a "rough copy edit" and can only occur after the manuscript has been evaluated for structural soundness. The line editing process does not aim to correct every minor error but rather to continue building on the manuscript's consistency as a whole. The copy editor will check for ways to improve the tone and style to better match the manuscript's goals. If fact-checking needs to occur, the line editing phase is where that will happen. The line reader should fact check information such as places, links, events, and references provided in the manuscript to ensure that the statements are correct. If the manuscript needs an index, it will require a separate "editing pass," which can be done by an indexer or by the line editor.

Addressing Structural Inconsistencies

The role of the line editor is to catch any structural issues which may have been overlooked. If there are remaining structural errors, the manuscript may require further structural editing. The line editor must bear in mind the manual guide chosen for the document to ensure that all of the content is per this manual. The line editor will rely on the style sheet to ensure consistency and add to the style sheet. The style sheet serves as an outline for rules concerning punctuation, spelling, acronyms, capitalization, fonts, and heading and is crucial for creating dependability within the manuscript.

Catching Major Spelling, Punctuation, and Grammatical Errors

As the line editor proceeds through the editing process, they have the authority to make grammatical changes, move sentences and paragraphs around, select deletion of repetitive information, and suggest rewrites for sentences and paragraphs. Their goal is to catch the significant spelling and punctuation errors to improve the grammar of the manuscript.

Conducting Editing Passes

In many cases, the manuscript will pass through a variety of line editing stages. Each stage is considered an 'editing pass,' Each manuscript requires a different number of passes to ensure that all significant corrections have been made. The line editor's role does not extend to correcting minor errors; however, more minor errors may be encountered as the manuscript goes through more passes.

Creating the Final Copy Edit

The final stage of the copyediting process is the most meticulous of all. It is the final stage of corrections before the final design and proofreading stages before publication. If the writing will not be published, the 'final copy edit' is the final stage of the editing process. The stakes are high in this stage, and the process is more detailed.

When copyediting things like newsletters, applications, and reports, which are not going to be published, the copy editor can assume that the document has already undergone self-editing and should not address too many errors. The copy editor strives to catch the last remaining grammatical, punctuation, or spelling errors that were not detected during the initial editing stages.

In the case of a manuscript that will be published, it must receive a final copy edit before it is sent into the final stages of design and proofreading before publication. Manuscripts that need this last copy edit before the designing stage are fiction or nonfiction manuscripts, annual reports, or any other report that will be distributed publicly.

Checking the Manuscript with Fresh Eyes

The copy editor's role is to catch any basic editing that was missed in the line editing stage, using the style sheet and any other manual guides for reference on appropriate stylistic decisions. With fresh eyes, the copy editor will correct any minor mistakes that have not previously been addressed. They will check for any inconsistencies in the text and deal with information such as appendices, index, publication information, and the table of contents that have not been addressed by the line editor.

Preparing for the Final Stage

After the first copy editing pass occurs, the copy editor will work with the author to determine if it is sufficient or needs to go through another pass to ensure no errors. Before the document is turned in or passed on to the design stage, the copy editor must be able to confirm with confidence that there are no errors, and the document is fully ready for the following step.

Chapter 2: Step 2 - Reading Work Aloud

Have you ever been trying to edit an essay with a peer or teacher and been told to "Try reading it aloud?" This is a common editing strategy because it pulls us out of the space of skimming and forces us to engage with the text differently. The process of reading aloud can serve as a useful tool to catch the areas that seem "off" but can be easily ignored when reading the text in your head.

Reading aloud not only builds continuity and confidence with what has been written, but it also helps you to engage with the meaning differently, comprehend what is on the paper, identifying the writing voice, and establishing areas where the flow could be improved.

Significant Benefits of Reading Aloud

There are several significant benefits to reading aloud. The first is that the process of reading aloud helps you to hone in on dialogue and narrative, capture its real authenticity, and ensure that all the right characters are speaking at the right time to keep things flowing. Reading aloud is visual and helps paint a picture in your mind as you read the text, leading you to make changes or say more in some text regions to make these images more potent for the reader.

Reading aloud also yields a more remarkable ability for self-expression. If you are the writer and the editor of your own piece, reading aloud can help establish the connection between your speaking and writing voice. Additionally, reading aloud helps build on your internal listening skills, which can help you tune in to the writing voice of yourself (if you are editing your own work) or the writer you are working for. This can yield more significant success in future writings.

Editing for Clarity and Correctness

In terms of editing for clarity and correctness, reading aloud helps you to sound out words, catch stumbling blocks created by poor punctuation, detect the use of syllables, and catch misspellings. It is much easier to tell if a sentence is a run-on or a word is misspelled if you have the chance to verbalize it. Not only is reading aloud the best way to establish fluidity, build connections, and catch otherwise unnoticeable errors in the text you edit, it can also develop your skills in public speaking.

Reading Aloud as a First Step

When it comes to editing your writing, reading aloud is crucial in catching the mistakes that become easy to miss. As soon as you finish writing your piece, it's a good idea to read it aloud before doing anything else. This is an excellent tactic for catching some initial structural and grammatical errors right from the beginning, which will make the rest of the process much more comfortable. As you read the writing aloud, keep a pen or highlighter handy that you can use to mark areas where you notice yourself stumbling or feeling confused at what was just said.

Establishing Text Flow

When you read aloud, you can establish how your writing flows, how a particular section works (or doesn't work) with the next, and if you are staying in the active voice. One of the best ways to catch passivity is through the reading aloud process. If you find yourself stumbling or getting lost on the message of what you're reading, that is a clear sign that edits are needed.

As you read your work aloud, it becomes clearer whether or not the correct punctuation marks are being used. If you notice pauses, questions, or exclamations in your oral reading, there is reason to believe you should either insert a comma or add a period. If you find yourself going on and on in a single sentence, that's a good sign that sentence is a run-on and needs to be broken up. By listening to your pauses, you can better avoid punctuation errors and run-on sentences. The read-aloud also gives you a process to question your grammar and the meaning of the work. If you don't know what you're reading about, your other readers certainly will not.

Deepening Reader Understanding

To that same token, if you find yourself growing bored as you read, it's a good sign that a particular section needs to be cut.

Boredom while reading is usually a result of the momentum slowing down too much or the writing theme becoming lost to leave the reader asking, "What's going on here and what's the point?" If you feel like a specific section of the writing is slow or confusing, it should either be changed or cut out entirely.

Verbalizing as a Thinking Tool

Saying things out loud about your writing can also be helpful when it comes to remembering ideas for later. If you have an idea but can't write it down, speak it into existence. Listening to yourself talk about it can help form the idea into a memory that you can later take back to your writing desk. Similarly, as you come up with new ideas of things to write or elements to add to your pieces, talk the ideas through with yourself beforehand. It's a good idea to speak these ideas out loud, ask yourself questions the reader may ask, work through inconsistencies and unclear parts, and genuinely engage with the dialogue. In doing this, you can already bring an outside voice to your writing, which can help eliminate ideas that won't get you very far and encourage you to think more.

Personifying Dialogue

Because dialogue is a verbal exchange between multiple characters, the only way to truly measure its efficiency is by verbalizing it. One way to do this is by viewing the dialogue like that of a script. As you read, pay attention to how natural and authentic the dialogue sounds. Does it sound rigid or overly rehearsed? Is each line being spoken necessary? Is there more that needs to be said? Does the correct character talk about each line, or should someone else be saying it? To keep your readers engaged, you must establish this sense of engagement in yourself by reading aloud.

Making Pace Adjustments

Reading your work aloud helps with pacing as it gives you an idea of which parts of the writing are fast-pasted and engaging and where things slow down. Once you have this knowledge, you can question whether or not certain areas are moving too quickly and trying to tackle too much (which can leave the reader feeling confused and strung along) or if they are too slow (which can leave the reader feeling bored and uninspired).

Using your pen or highlighting tool, mark the areas where you notice significant differences in the pacing, and ask yourself if each scene is correctly paced or would be more potent if it was slowed down or sped up. Slowing things down can help the reader take a break from something hectic that just happened or build tension for something wild that is about to happen. Reading aloud is the only way to catch these pacing details.

Honing in on Important Details

Along with improving your pacing, reading aloud also serves to enhance the flow of the writing. As mentioned previously, it is easy for our brains to skip over the seemingly minute details to get to the point of what we are reading. This is especially true if you have been looking at the same piece of writing repeatedly. At some point, your subconscious begins to ignore the finer details. Eventually, even as you read aloud, you may find yourself trying to skip words or move things around. Make a note of these things and ask yourself if your natural desire to do this warrants some sort of change in the text.

Establishing Specific Areas to Edit

Hearing the work you have written read aloud often brings things to light that are hard to notice as our eyes repeatedly scan the page. In the early editing stages specifically, there is a lot more work to be done than we may realize. The writing may be too wordy, too fast, too slow, or lack emotion and passion, have inefficient dialogue, or simply lack interest level. If you are a writer who plans to send your manuscript to an editor to work with, be sure to read it aloud and sort through things first. This way, you can provide more input to your editor on what you need help with. If you are the editor of someone else's work, encourage them to read it aloud beforehand so they can provide more of a basis for discussion. Once it is in your hands, continue to read it aloud until everything sounds right.

Reading Aloud to Others

The final step of reading work aloud in the editing process is to read aloud to another person (or people). The person you read in front of can be anyone from a close friend, family member, or partner, to a peer or even a stranger. Regardless of who you choose to read aloud to, you can rely on the innate appreciation of social behavior to increase your desire to solve problems and pay more in-depth attention to the writing.

Reading aloud is typically a more vulnerable and intimidating experience, especially if you read something you wrote yourself. When we read material aloud, our natural social instincts become heightened because we know other people listen to us and draw opinions from what we say. We have an innate desire to perform well in front of others and receive positive feedback. Your responses will be heightened from this space of vulnerability and slight nervousness, and you may notice things you began to ignore in previous readings subconsciously. You will be extra sensitive to inconsistencies in pace, rhythm, and flow, as well as if a particular section drones on for too long. This heightened sensitivity will allow you to make even more changes and come closer to perfection than you could be reading only to yourself. In this state, you will also have a deeper appreciation for the writing structure, and your desire to produce a pleasing effect will increase.

The heightened sensitivity and social pressure of reading aloud to another person will make the errors in grammar, flow, and punctuation leap out even further, as you will feel nervous about making mistakes. You will be likely to look upon the writing with more meticulous eyes as you consider the fact that other listeners are drawing their conclusions and making their judgments. This will motivate you to solve the problems you encounter within the text as quickly and efficiently as possible.

Chapter 3: Step 3 - Setting Things Apart

When it comes to elements like headings, captions, indexes, appendixes, tables, and contents lists, it can be hard to stay focused. Writers tend to focus more on the main point of what they are trying to say, the characters they develop, and what they want the reader to take away. It is typical for the seemingly fewer essential elements of the writing to slip through the cracks. With the competition of the writing industry and the bustling state of the world, editors cannot afford to be careless with these elements.

Giving Readers Something to Skim

As people navigate their busy lives, they are more likely to skim through writing than profoundly engaging from start to finish. To capture the reader's attention, you must be concise and convincing, drawing them to slow down and engage more deeply with what is being said. When a customer is looking for a piece of content to contend with, they are not reading page after page of the writing itself. Instead, they are looking at the headings, captions, indexes, appendixes, tables, and contents lists to tell them more about what to expect and help them decide if it is worth their time. If a reader is confused by the headings and cannot figure out what will be said in each section, they will have no desire to read that section.

However, if they see even one or two headers that specifically pique their interest, they will be more likely to read on. Readers will be turned off by sloppy captions as well, whereas well-written captions will help them engage further with the content from the start.

Additionally, readers can become overwhelmed by overly detailed indexes or disengaged with overly brief indexes. Although these elements seem small, they serve as the signposts that allow the writer to communicate the purpose of the text, summarize, and highlight the key takeaways. That said, each of these elements is crucial for slowing a reader down in their tracks and drawing them into what the writer has to say. The engagement with these elements should compose at least half of the editing journey.

Tying up Loose Ends

As the editor (of your work or someone else's), it is your job to tie up loose ends and ensure the presented content is clear and well-supported. The hope of every editor of someone else's writing is that the writer will have done some of this work on their own first (for example, by reading aloud).

However, this is not always the case; as many times, the writer will have burnt out from the writing process and will feel that they cannot look at the text any longer. As the editor, you must be able to work with the content in hand, no matter what state it is in. In the cases of editors working for clients, this may look like doing the "dirty work" the writer did not have the energy to do—writing the copy for headings, captions, or any other missing elements. If you are both the writer and the editor, you must be able to enter into a new space in the editing process, in which you are prepared to take on this "dirty work" with a fresh mind.

Conducting Regular Check-ins

After you have checked for grammatical errors, punctuation errors, and spelling errors in the main text, it is good to check for the same things in things like the major headings and the names of people in the manuscript. This check-over should occur in both the manuscript and proofing stages, as errors can be missed even with several editing passes. The last thing you want to happen is to catch these errors once a piece of writing is already published, and the only way to avoid this is by being as meticulous as possible in the editing stages.

Writing Headings and Subheadings

Headings and subheadings must be consistent with pre-established formatting, and they should all look the same (same font, same size, same position, same general length). In general, these elements of all main headings such as chapter titles, 'Contents,' 'Preface,' 'Index,' and 'Appendix' should follow the same model. These headings should be organized logically, separating the text into easy-to-follow sections. Titles should usually have more space above than below them, with spacing varying slightly depending on the heading's importance (for example, a critical heading may be provided with more space, have a larger font sized, and be centered with more space than the average subheading).

Essential articles are marked by the most massive headlines, which should be placed near the top of the page to avoid imbalance. Another tip is to use short words in headings and subheadings as often as possible to avoid confusion that can arise from overusing hyphens.

Not only do headings and subheadings need to be correctly formatted and consistent with one another, but they also need to grab the reader's attention and make them want to read on. In many cases, the writing draft may have some headings in place by the time they reach the editing stage. However, just because the titles exist does not mean they are influential or will serve the purpose of drawing readers closer. Publications will be more successful if they have headers that make a clear statement, impress advertisers, and keep readers feeling hungry for more. If this job is not accomplished in the first drafts, it is the editor's job to rewrite the headers to make it so.

Writing and Editing Captions

When it comes to editing captions, you must remember that even if readers are not engaging deeply with the text's body, they will be naturally drawn to images and pieces of text set apart from the rest in caption form. Captions should be kept short and relevant and should be conclusive with what is happening in the illustration and the surrounding body text. Ideally, the reader will be able to understand what is happening on the page by merely examining a clear-cut caption. As the editor, you must be aware of any cross-references in the text which correspond to illustrations and make sure the figure numbers in the captions line up. It is best to use as few page numbers in cross-references as possible to save yourself the cost and the possibility of requiring further edits.

Dividing the Process into Stages

If you're feeling overwhelmed by the intensity of the editing process, don't worry. There are undoubtedly many things to consider, and the stakes are high for catching as many edits as possible to avoid misprints and ensure the publications' success. That said, there is an excellent technique for keeping yourself on track and preventing overwhelm in the editing stage. This technique involves splitting up each of these "smaller elements" of the writing and focusing on them one at a time. Start with the headings. Confer with your guidelines on which font style, size, and spacing to use in the titles and subheadings, and check them through for consistency. After you have gone over the headings several times, move on to captions. Once again, confer with the guidelines for caption writing.

With each caption, ask yourself if it is clear, concise, and in line with what is happening in the image and the rest of the text. After captions, move on to tables and content lists. Make sure the content lists direct readers to where they need to go to find specific information. As for the tables, make sure the information provided highlights the text's main points or provides the reader with necessary background information (like statistics of case studies).

Next, move on to the index and appendix. Check each one to ensure it contains just the right amount of detail, not too much, and not too little. By breaking up each of these steps and dedicating time to each, you are more likely to catch inconsistencies.

Chapter 4: Step 4 - Utilizing Isolation Strategies

As you move through the editing process, it may become gradually more difficult to tell one idea of the text from the next. After a while, words begin to meld together, and the overall context may become muddled. To keep a clear perspective with each text block, you need to be proactive with text isolation strategies. Later in the guide, we will explore further strategies for maintaining clarity, such as taking space from the text and reading in reverse. However, these strategies generally take place after the manuscript has undergone several editing passes. For this chapter, we will focus on methods of text isolation in the early stages of editing.

Keeping the Focus

Throughout the initial editing process, it can be helpful to use a blank sheet of paper to cover the text you have not yet reviewed. By doing this, you can keep your attention focused on the text at hand instead of looking ahead or becoming distracted. As you finish reading specific paragraphs, make a mark to show that you have looked at them, and don't go back until you are in the next full editing pass.

Breaking the Text into Sections

Another strategy of isolation goes hand-in-hand with the concept of taking space. Depending on your project's length, it is a good idea to establish how you will break up the text before beginning your editing process. It is very difficult to be thorough in the copyediting stages if you don't create small "cut off points" or benchmarks to keep you on track. If you are editing a poem of six stanzas with four lines in each stanza, it would be smart to give yourself about half an hour to work with the material.

Take about four minutes per stanza, with one minute dedicated to each line. You can use this minute to read the line aloud, isolated from all the rest of the poem, to check for flow and word choice. After you have finished all four lines of a particular stanza, take one minute to evaluate the stanza as a whole. Take a moment to breathe, then move on to the following stanza.

Considering Interest Level and Familiarity

On the other hand, if you are editing a 300-page book, the process of text isolation will look much different. You should begin by asking yourself how easy or challenging this particular content is for you to edit. Is it a topic you're familiar with, or is it entirely new knowledge that may take longer to process and could require additional research? Is it something that piques your interest, or is it out of your general interest area and could become tedious as you go along? Is the book written for young audiences and will be a quick and easy read, or is it designed to be intellectually challenging and maybe more time consuming to get through?

Knowing the answer to all of these questions ahead of time will make it much easier for you to understand how to divide the text into isolated sections. Not only will this allow you to be more thorough, but it will also make the process of editing much more manageable. Once you have determined the project's density and your interest level and familiarity, it's time to develop a system for breaking up the text.

Working Through Sections Quickly

If you are familiar with the content in the 300-page book and find it reasonably interesting, you will likely be able to work faster. In this case, you may choose to divide the 300-pages up into ten sections of ten pages, which you can read through fairly quickly. In between each area, take a brief break to look away from the text you just read, leaving it in the past as you move on to a new isolated piece of text. During this break, you may choose to be on your phone, use the restroom, or take a drink of water. Regardless of what you do, make sure to clear your head of the text you just read (besides the general context that you will need to take with you), and allow yourself to move on fully to the next piece.

Determining How Many Sections to Read Per Day

Once you've developed a general system of section-lengths and subsequent breaks, you can decide how many sections to read per day. If each section of ten pages takes fifteen minutes to read, you may choose to do the work in two days, putting in 1-2 hours of work per day. With each isolated section of the text, be sure to give yourself a few moments to reflect upon what you just read, and make notes of your questions and observations to refer back to on the following editing pass.

Working Through Dense Content

If the 300-page book is dense content that is harder for you to understand or feel interested in, you can expect that it will take more time, and you may also need longer breaks in between. You may decide, for example, to divide the readings up into ten-page sections but give yourself 30-40 minutes to complete them. After sitting down for this amount of time to edit a ten-page section, you may find yourself ready for a more extended break, like having a meal, going to exercise, going to a meeting, or merely doing another activity. You can expect this project to be more slow-going and should propose your deadlines as such.

If the sections are denser and take more time and mental energy, you should expect to get through fewer sections each day. Ultimately, it is best to take the time you need to make thorough edits of each isolated area, analyze that section, and carefully write down any notes you have instead of trying to power through the text.

Chapter 5: Step 5 - Interacting for Deeper Engagement

One of the best ways to stay engaged with the editing process is to interact with the text. Interacting with the text can take on numerous forms, from making physical marks on punctuation, grammar, and spelling, to taking a creative spin on reading the story from various character's perspectives. As the editor, it is your job to be fully engaged with the texts at all times, sometimes even more than the writer was. Passivity is a grave mistake in an editor and should be avoided at all costs.

The editor must be a reader who can avoid surface level word processing and truly gain something from the text, to offer meaningful feedback in return. In general, interacting with the text helps editors to avoid falling into passive reading and maintain high activity as they go along. This may look like using the imagination, wondering about further possibilities, asking questions, making analyses and evaluations, and otherwise thinking deeply. Through these tactics, editors will have higher levels of comprehension of what they read. Therefore, they will be able to offer more meaningful edits and suggestions to the writer (or make more meaningful edits to their own writing if they are the writer).

Benefits of Deep Text Interaction

There are several benefits to more in-depth interaction with the text in the editing stages, all of which help make the piece of writing as clear, concise, engaging, and error-free as possible. This deeper interaction helps the editor to think deeply about what they are reading and pinpoint when they feel confused or find themselves drifting off. If the editor feels confused at a certain point in the text, that's a good sign that the author needs to re-work that section of text for clarification purposes.

If the editor begins to drift off and has trouble paying attention to the words in front of them, that's a good sign that the writer should move that section of the text, add more colorful language, or remove it entirely. Text interaction helps to fill in any gaps in comprehension and urge the editor to reflect on both what they have taken from the text and what they anticipate for the future.

Physical Interaction Method

The first method of text interaction is physical interaction. This comes through editing methods, which keep the editor's brain engaged in a particular action system. An example of this would be to develop a table of individual edits to apply to punctuation, grammatical, and spelling errors. Perhaps the editor chooses to place an "x" symbol over every area of the text where there is an unnecessary comma, a circle around areas lacking punctuation, three lines under letters that are incorrectly capitalized, and short underlines under words that should be removed or changed. They may choose to underline or bracket the sentences or sections that capture their attention the most and circle the sentences or paragraphs to find themselves feeling lost or bored.

In terms of spelling, if the editor knows a word is misspelled, they may put it in a circle or box, and if they have questions about the spelling or meaning of a word, they may put a question mark. They could also use arrows to indicate where individual sentences should be moved.

Using a physical symbols system keeps the editor's brain on task while they work and helps them keep from getting lost when they try to refer back to the text. It also gives the writer something to look at so they can see all of the places in the text where the editor found issues. This physical interaction provides the editor with something to do as they read, which is enjoyable and useful for keeping the process on track.

Physical interaction is a deliberate act and can be especially helpful if the editor is working with a piece that they do not find naturally attractive or challenging them more than usual. The physical actions may make the task less daunting, and the editor will have more confidence in what they can do.

Personal Interaction Method

Another method of interaction is personal interaction. To do this, the editor may take the approach of building personal connections with the text by relating it to their own experience or understanding of the world. They may engage with the text by asking particular questions of themselves, such as: "How do I feel when I read this scene?" "What are my emotions towards this character?" "Whose side am I on/Who am I rooting for?" "What do I want the outcome of this piece of writing to be?" "Am I pleased with what just happened in this scene?" "What is confusing to me about this scene?" "What have I learned from this piece of writing?" "What new perspective have I gained?".

It's a good idea to make a list of questions such as these for the editor to answer as they go along. By building these personal connections, the editor will begin to feel like there is more at stake for themselves and their personal life. Their interest levels will be higher, and they will be more intentional and less likely to become distracted. Additionally, their answers to these questions should indicate whether or not the writer has done their job.

Every editor should approach their editing projects with the goal of reading to learn. They should comprehensively analyze the text, integrate new ideas and perceptions, and offer feedback that stems from a place of genuine interest and understanding of what the writer wants to convey.

Chapter 6: Step 6 - Letting Things Sit

Most editors have had the experience of growing bored with the piece of writing in front of them and growing exhausted from reading the same characters, dialogues, and scenes over and over again. This is called burnout, and as an editor, you can almost certainly expect it to happen to you. Editing can be a tedious process, especially once you're a few editing passes in. This is a natural and normal part of the process, but it is not productive. Once you have reached this point, the best way to get back on track is to grant yourself time to step away. Go out and live your life for a few hours, a day, or a few days, without having to think about the editing project at hand. Give yourself a chance to read, engage with other things you enjoy, relax, watch the people and things going on around you, and gain some fresh perspective.

When you come back to the editing process, you can do so with "fresh eyes" and a new perspective for the content in front of you. With this fresh perspective, you will not only enjoy the process more and feel more energized; you will also be able to catch things you did not notice before and offer new critiques. In some cases, you may even find yourself suggesting the writer bring in an entirely new idea or change the focus of individual sections entirely.

Choosing to Take a Break When Frustrated

Looking over the same piece of writing over and over can cause the work to become stale. No editor is unfamiliar with the feeling that comes when you're sitting at your desk, looking at the same project, and nothing is coming forth. Although you know you should have more to say and that there are undoubtedly more edits to make, nothing is coming to you. It is expected that you will start to feel tired throughout the editing process and have trouble focusing as you read the same section for the third or fourth time. You may find yourself beginning to feel frustrated and not know how much more you can do. You may also be dealing with a flustered writer (or, perhaps, you are this flustered writer) who just can't seem to find what "works."

Frustration is usually a good sign that it is time to take a step back. If you find yourself losing sight of the purpose of the writing and the enjoyment in the process of editing it, you will benefit the most from giving yourself a break. If you feel like you have to force yourself through every page, give yourself space from the text to think about what isn't working, get back in touch with your creativity, restore your energy, and bring back some fresh ideas.

Choosing to take a break can save you hours of staring at a screen or page and not comprehending any of the words in front of you. When you take a step back, take some time to remind yourself of the writer's (or your own) purpose in writing this piece. Ask yourself, "What's the point?" and give yourself time to meditate on that while you take a break from it. It's also important not to make yourself miserable throughout the writing process. If you start to feel yourself continuously wrapped up in negative emotions from the stress of editing, do yourself a favor and give yourself some time to rest, breathe, and do things that bring you joy.

Tuning into Your Surroundings

One method for giving your editing space while still gathering perspectives, which will be beneficial when you return, is to tune in to your surroundings when you go out. While you are taking your break from editing, pay particular attention to the people you see around you at the grocery store, in the park, at the mall, or on the streets.

Watch the way they interact with each other; note the way they use body language and the way they engage in daily dialogue. Suppose you're editing a piece of writing that involves character dialogue. In that case, you can take inspiration from the real world to see if the dialogue you're editing sounds realistic and flows well or if it sounds unnatural and hard to follow. As you listen to everyday people engage in conversation, you may realize that some of the dialogue in the piece you're editing sounds too formal or boring. The natural world is full of inspiration, and taking a break to simply inhabit the world can be revolutionary to your editing style.

Strengthening Character Development from Real-World People

This observation of everyday people can also give you more insight to offer the writer on how to develop their characters. You may have the idea of realistic descriptions to add to a particular character to make them seem more relatable, an action they can take that would surprise the reader, etc. You may even have an idea for a new character goal, or a new character entirely, which you can present to the writer (or bring into the piece yourself if you are the writer). Observing a couple in love on a park bench, the exact way they touch each other, how they move their heads to look at each other, and how they speak could form the way you reframe such a circumstance as you edit the writing.

You may see an older woman in the supermarket who reminds you of one of the characters in the piece you are editing. You can take down some brief observations to bring into her character description to become more realistic. As you discreetly observe body language and general human interactions, you may be able to provide further tips for the writer to create scenes the readers can visualize and relate to. The more the reader can visually see what is happening and establish a sense of interest and relatability with the characters, the more inclined they will be to continue reading.

You can play into this interest level by relating the characters in the work you're editing to people you see in your everyday life. If you are editing a piece of writing that involves a motorcyclist named Haven, for example, and you see a woman in a café who rides a motorcycle and reminds you of how the character of Haven may be in real life, you can draw inspiration from the way she drinks her coffee, the tattoos on her arms, etc. In this way, simple observation of real human beings can revolutionize character development and improvement in the editing stage.

Reading for Other Purposes

Another essential thing to do while taking your break from editing is to engage with other author's writing. In many cases, you cannot engage with work you are editing as you would if it were merely a book you picked up off the shelf. The content may be something that is not interesting to you, or you may simply not be able to feel interested because you have too much work to do with finding errors and making suggestions. For this reason, it is crucial always to have something you are reading for pure enjoyment and learning, rather than editing.

As you read the work of other authors you enjoy, ask yourself questions like, "What about this piece of writing captures my attention, and how does the author maintain it?" "Do I care about the characters in this story? If so, why do I care? If not, why not?" "How does the author keep this story moving forward and keep me from becoming bored?" You can improve your editing skills drastically by understanding the techniques used by the authors you like and making similar suggestions to the authors you work with (or applying them to your writing). If you or the author feel like the piece of writing needs something more but can't progress beyond where it is, you can use other writers' work to remind yourself how to bring in extra elements that maintain reader interest.

Move the Mind, Move the Body

Most writers and editors will tell you that moving the body is crucial, especially when your brain is constantly active. Sometimes, your thoughts will become so chaotic and activated that they don't know where to go, and it can become hard to continue the editing process in this state. Mental and physical activity go hand in hand, and you indeed cannot have one without the other. Exercise keeps our brains clear, our moods positive, and our emotions even, which are all critical throughout the editing process's challenges. In many cases, sitting down to edit after a workout is excellent because your mind will be crystal clear, your endorphins will be freely flowing, and you will likely feel more in control and ready to tackle your task.

Editing is a stressful process, and exercise is the perfect way to release that buildup of stress. This doesn't need to get a gym membership or join the community sand volleyball league; it merely means you need to find the way that works best for you to move your body and use it (especially during the editing process). In many cases, a nice jog, yoga practice, dance workout video, or walk around the neighborhood can be the perfect release of endorphins and a way to refocus your brain for when you come back to editing. Whatever type of exercise it takes for you to release your stress, clear your head, and revive your energy, give yourself time to step away and do it.

Giving Yourself Adequate Time

In every step of the editing process, it is important to give yourself plenty of time. If you rush your deadlines and set crunched timelines for yourself, you will not be able to be as clear-headed and thorough. Ultimately, this will result in a less refined piece of writing. While it is easy to become so caught up in the editing process that you feel desperate just to get it done, this can pose a great threat to the work's quality. Be sure not to short yourself on time. Editing is a process that cannot be rushed, and you need to allow for plenty of space to take breaks to make the most intentional edits possible. If you're wondering how long your breaks should be or how much time you should request to meet your editing deadlines, remember that the writing will ultimately benefit from any space you take away from it.

Try your best to keep guilty feelings at bay and value your own time, energy, and general enjoyment in the process. If you are editing for another writer, it is important to have a transparent conversation with them about the importance of breaks and taking space from the writing. Clarify your needs and why you are setting a particular deadline. This will help the author understand your process, which will ultimately put less pressure on you and allow you to do your absolute best.

Redirecting Energy on the "Off Days"

If you sit down to write one day and you feel overwhelmed by negative emotions, lack of motivation, or general disinterest, it's probably not a day you should be writing. In a society that is very driven towards production and meeting deadlines, it's hard to believe it would be okay to change your plans on a day you planned to edit. However, if you don't feel like this is the right day for you to do hours of editing, it probably isn't.

With good planning, you can provide this flexibility for yourself. It's okay for today not to be the right day to edit the way you planned. Instead, decide how you're going to spend the day giving yourself a break, re-cultivating your interest, and drawing interest from the world around you. Just because you're not doing the editing in your traditional process doesn't mean you can't gain experience from reading, taking notes of the things you observe in the world around you, and giving yourself time for the things you need and the things that bring you relaxation and joy. Editing is a draining process, and the more drained you become, the less quality work you will perform. If you sit down and realize today isn't the day for editing, allow yourself to step away, redirecting that energy to a place where it can be productive, then come back tomorrow.

Planning Breaks Ahead of Time

On a typical editing day, it's not a good idea to sit down for hours at a time and try to get everything done. If you do this, your brain may become desensitized to issues with style or other edits that need to be made and start automatically filling in the gaps that need your attention. If you plan to write for four hours, it's a good idea to decide how long your breaks will be within that period. Even if you take just five minutes every hour to stand up, stretch, drink some water, or step outside for a breath of air, your writing process will thank you immensely. You may also try an approach where you write for several hours a day for two days, then take a day to step away. In some cases, however, you may need even longer. Deadlines permitting, you may need to step away for several weeks or even months.

This is especially useful if you are trying to edit your writing and find yourself hitting walls. Give yourself time to live your life, and during that time, you'll be surprised at the new observations, perspective, and energy to bring back to the editing process when you're ready.

Chapter 7: Step 7 - Editing in Reverse

Let's say you have read and edited the same piece of writing several times, and you're beginning to hit a wall. You know that there is more to do, but you can't quite figure it out. You have indicated the writer's main goals, determined where the tension and crisis points are, paid attention to the momentum at various points throughout, made basic grammatical, spelling, and punctuation edits, checked for consistency and clarity, and even read the manuscript aloud. All of the standard editing boxes are checked, yet you still feel that something is missing. This is where editing in reverse comes in.

Overcoming Preconceptions, Deepening Concentration

As discussed previously, your brain automatically fills in the gaps as you edit. When it isn't necessary to focus on every word to get the text's main point, it's common to miss places where the flow is not as smooth as it should be, words are misspelled, or faulty punctuation is used. Putting things in reverse (meaning starting with the last sentence and making your way up) helps to hone your focus on each word and sentence in a new way.

Editing in reverse forces your brain to confront what feels like entirely new information. You will have to slow down and read each word and sentence as if it is the first time you've ever seen it. In many ways, it is the first time you've ever seen it because by reading in a different order, you are automatically unable to operate under the same unconscious assumptions of the plot. The more comfortable you are with the flow of the story and the plot, the more likely you'll be to miss problem areas. Reading in reverse allows you to disrupt this comfort, go against your unconscious assumptions, and genuinely engage with the text with fresh eyes.

When you start from the end, your brain can't assume that "we already know all this," and you will therefore be able to be much more thorough. Each paragraph you read will become an entity that stands alone, which allows you to be more intentional as you examine the sentence structure and words. As you read more slowly and with greater intention and challenge, you will be more deliberate in your editing. Your concentration will deepen, and you will notice the flow of each paragraph in a way you did not before.

Beginning at the End

When you begin the process of editing in reverse, you will want to start at the very end of the manuscript. You may choose to read the pages in the standard order, from top to bottom, but you can read from bottom to top if you want an even more significant editing challenge. By taking each page and paragraph out of context you have become familiar with, you will have to look at each word and phrase and ask yourself what it accomplishes. You will want to make corrections as you go, marking up the paper or making notes in the margins. If you have a new idea for a sentence structure, try it out in the margins. If you're not sure about a correction, feel free to indicate your uncertainty using parentheses or a question mark so you can refer back later on in the editing process.

As you move through the paragraphs, you may choose to choose some method of indicating that you have finished a paragraph, so you don't look at again until the next editing pass. You may highlight a section, mark it with an asterisk, or something else of the sort.

Correcting Consistency, Punctuation, Grammar, and Spelling

Editing in reverse gives you more ability to identify inconsistencies within the text. You may find, for example, that a character is present in a scene they shouldn't be in, or perhaps that a scene is placed in the wrong order. You're more likely to catch these things if you're reading the text in a different way than you're used to. Some of the other things you'll be looking for in the reverse editing stage are punctuation, spelling, and grammar errors.

Identifying Overuse

However, there are several other emphasis areas you should keep in mind, as well. The first of these is the overuse of certain words. Every writer has words they overuse, which can cause the manuscript to lose its flavor. As you read through the manuscript in reverse, highlight, or underline every time the writer uses a similar word. Perhaps they overuse the adjective "beautiful", or the phrase "That being said." After identifying the overused words and phrases, you can easily use a Google search or another simple tool to identify supplementary words and phrases the writer could use instead.

Identifying "Non" Words

Another thing to look out for in the reverse editing process is the use of "non" words. These are the words that can easily be removed without changing anything about the sentence meaning. In many cases, these words are "dead" to the sentence, meaning they make it less impactful and break the flow. There are thousands of "non" words out there, with the words "just," "really," and "very" being just a few.

Drafting in Reverse

In addition to editing in reverse, many editors also find it helpful to draft a reverse outline to check the work. The process of reversal outlining involves taking away all supporting evidence and details and leaving yourself with only the writer's main ideas. You should be able to define these main ideas using bullet-points, which you should ensure are placed in a logical order. This provides a condensed version of the piece of writing, in which the writer can confront if all of their goals have genuinely been met in their main points. After you have generated a reverse outline of the main points you gathered in the editing process, the writer will better understand the places where they need to provide more evidence, expand or condense a scene, or move things around for better organization.

Keeping Author Goals in Mind

The reverse outline cannot be created until the writer has completed a draft and provided it to you to describe their goals. Once you are aware of the goals, you can proceed through the manuscript with a sense of alertness about what is being accomplished in each chapter and paragraph. Before you begin editing, ask the author to present you with a basic outline that lists their writing's main ideas as they understand them. This outline will serve as something to refer back to throughout the editing process and give you something to question. As you begin making your reverse outline, consider using numbers with each bulleted point to keep yourself on track with which paragraph or chapter talks about what.

Answering Crucial Questions

The most critical point of a reverse outline is to answer questions. As you go through each paragraph, section, or chapter, ask yourself if they accurately relate to the author's expressed goals. This strategy will help you catch any scenes or pieces of information that seem irrelevant to the big picture and end up de-railing readers. As you proceed throughout the reverse outlining process, you may find yourself confronting new topics or ideas which are presented throughout the paper and may not relate to the main idea. In this case, the author either needs to change the main idea of the writing itself or remove the irrelevant information.

Another question you should ask yourself throughout the reverse outlining process is where the reader may have trouble feeling on track with the points' order. Are there areas where they may be confused chronologically or feel that they need more information? By asking this question, you can make editing suggestions for how the writer might rearrange the manuscript or individual paragraphs themselves to keep the reader feeling on track and tied into the writing's central theme(s).

As you examine each paragraph, make sure that you do not have any sections repeating the same idea. Although each paragraph should be relevant to the main idea, they should all say something new. If you have two paragraphs saying almost the same thing, it will help combine them, remove one, or revise so that they are each making a different point.

Editing the Specifics of Each Paragraph

It is also essential to make sure that each paragraph stays focused on a single topic. The writer should not try to cover too much ground in a single section; if they do, the reader will more easily get lost. If you identify paragraphs which try to tackle too many things, suggest that the writer separate those ideas to form further paragraphs, or cut the information out if it is not entirely relevant. Lastly, check each section for length requirements. Are they too long or too short? An excellent way to gauge this is by looking at the total number of pages. The longer the piece of writing, the less of a problem it is to have a few longer paragraphs. That said, it is vital to check each paragraph in-depth to make sure that it fits with the flow of the rest of the piece.

Conclusion

When you started this guide, you likely approached it as either the editor of another writer's work or with the desire to edit your writing thoroughly. You picked up this guide with the understanding that in-depth editing is crucial to the overall success of the piece that is being written and that errors in structure, clarity, punctuation, grammar, dialogue, and flow can have a drastically negative impact on how others receive your writing. You were likely aware of all that is at stake in the editing process, especially when it comes to maintaining the interest, understanding, and general respect of readers.

No matter how incredible a story's content is, too many spelling errors, grammatical mistakes, or inconsistencies can ruin the whole experience for a reader. When it comes to the editing stage, you must come prepared for the fact that how thorough you edit the book can make or break the levels of respect, and subsequent sales, it will have. When you edit your work, you should do so not only to create work you can be truly proud of, but also to cultivate a community of followers who have a deep respect for the work you produce.

Throughout the guide, you were provided with the ins and outs of the editing process, from the structural, line editing, and copywriting stages, to the importance of reading aloud, to the seemingly minor details of formatting, to deeply engaging with the content to a point where you can ensure reader impact. You became aware of the risks of missing small pieces if you become careless, and you learned how to be more thorough when it comes to catching these small pieces before it's too late.

You were provided with tips for keeping yourself engaged and present with the work you do. You also learned the benefits of creating a network of friends, followers, trusted writers, and perhaps other editors into your editing process for extra support and perspective. You learned how to maintain a fresh perspective while honoring your own energy by taking breaks, giving the writing space to breathe, taking inspiration from your surroundings, editing in reverse, and creating reverse outlines to clarify the author's main points.

You discovered the importance of being thorough and conducting as many editing passes as necessary to get the writing as close to perfect as possible. You were shown the benefits of reading work aloud to yourself and other people, because hearing it in your own voice can bring attention to details that are easy to skip while reading. You learned how to isolate parts of the text to scan for clarity and cohesivity, as well as how to step outside the original context of the text to slow down and hone in on the smaller details. Additionally, you came to understand some of the best editors' secrets and how to monitor your text for efficiency and full reader engagement.

At the end of the guide, you were provided with fresh ways to work with the text at hand to keep yourself alert and conscious of changes that still need to be made. This will help you save from being burnt out and becoming careless with your editing process. The better job you do as an editor, the more the reader will enjoy their engagement with it, and the more they will search for future pieces by you (or the writer you are editing for) in the future. No matter where you are on your editing journey, this guide is guaranteed to serve as the tool you need to keep yourself on track!

More by Jaiden Pemton

Discover all books from the Creative Writing Series by Jaiden Pemton at:

bit.ly/jaiden-pemton

Book 1: *How to Write Fiction*

Book 2: *How to Tell a Story*

Book 3: *How to Write a Screenplay*

Book 4: *How to Write Sales Copy*

Book 5: *How to Edit Writing*

Book 6: *How to Self-Publish*

Book 7: *How to Write Non-Fiction*

Book 8: *How to Write Content*

Themed book bundles available at discounted prices:

bit.ly/jaiden-pemton

9 798869 045614